TEI £17.99

Total Design
Managing the
design process
in the

This book is dedicated to Jaffa and Batman
whose moral and occasionally,
vocal support
sustained us during its writing.

The only way to type is with a cat on your lap.

Total Design
Managing the design process in the service sector

Gillian and Bill Hollins

Pitman

Pitman Publishing
128 Long Acre, London WC2E 9AN

A Division of Longman Group UK Limited

First published in 1991

British Library Cataloguing in Publication Data
Hollins, Gillian
    Managing the design process in the service sector.
    1. Production management
    I. Title II. Hollins, Bill
    658.5

ISBN: 0 273 03338 7

Typeset by Medcalf Type Ltd, Bicester, Oxon.
Printed in Great Britain by The Bath Press, Avon

Contents

Contents

Contents

List of figures

Preface

People involved in the production of new manufactured products have long appreciated the need for effective product design. More recently they have also understood that the design of successful products involves a process that needs to be managed. People involved in the service sector do not yet value the importance of good design nor appreciate how effective management can enhance their success in the market place.

Students undertaking management courses who are already working in, or have set their sights on a career in the service sector, are, initially, sceptical about the relevance of the management of innovation and design to them. It is not difficult to make them appreciate its importance.

It is now recognized that organizations require a continuing supply of new products to survive in an increasingly competitive world. The majority of new products are failures. One way to reduce this unacceptably high failure rate – in order to be better able to compete and succeed – is to consider product design as a total process, requiring a continuity of management input from the initial market research through to the eventual disposal of the product. This is called *Total Design*.

Until recently, the main thrust of research on how to organize the management of product design in organizations has been undertaken by engineers and has concerned manufactured products.

This book includes the findings of the first research undertaken on the step-by-step process of the design management of service products. It is the first book to explain how service products should be designed and how this design process should be managed. Other inputs have emanated from our consultancy. Furthermore, teaching postgraduates who, themselves, have a wealth of experience is a matter of two-way discussion. Their knowledge and practice have contributed greatly to this book.

The structure of this book provides a guide through the management of the provision of new service products. The main steps of total service product design are described. This identifies where mistakes most commonly occur – which is early in the design process – and how these mistakes can be avoided.

These early stages, or 'front end of design', are described in detail. Also discussed is who should be involved, how they should communicate and how they should be trained. A worked example of these early stages is given in the final chapter.

Although the techniques described in this book are the very latest of tried and tested methods, care has been taken to make this book easy to follow. It is, therefore, suitable for both the practitioner as well as those on management education courses.

We would also, finally, like to point out that for ease of expression we have used the masculine pronoun throughout. This should of course be taken to include both men and women in all instances.

About this book
and
service design

Chapter 1

Introduction

Why this book is needed

Services are products.
Products need to be designed.
Design is a process.
This process must be organized.
This organization is the job of management.

Nowadays most people are employed in the service sector. Services are like manufactured products in as much as they must be designed. In this book we will be talking about 'Total Design'. In Total Design all the stages of the process must be considered up to the eventual disposal of the product. In some texts Total Design is called 'integrated product design', or 'integrated design management' which can be considered the same thing.

Total Design involves a prescriptive almost rigid structure. Many experts are co-ordinated in this structure so that their skills are brought to bear on the various design problems at the 'right' time when they are most needed. This has been shown to result in more successful products in industry and these techniques are now applied to the service sector. All the major stages in the introduction of new products must be a success. If any one stage fails then the service offering will fail (*see* Fig. 1.1).

There are few prescriptive theories on how to manage design. In his summary of an International Conference on Design (ICED, 1985) Bruce Archer (1986) said:

Far too much of our work in this field . . . remains at too high a level of generality. We still make too many statements that are supported by a very low level of evidence, we have hardly any well founded theory.

I have spent some years working in and researching the management of product design, my main interest being total design. This involves much more

3

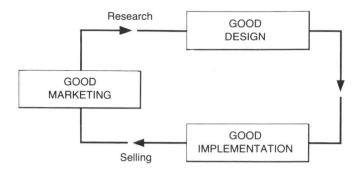

Fig. 1.1 All aspects of a new product innovation must be a success.

than just the area covered by those traditionally called 'designers'. Design should have a much wider scope – market research, production, accountancy and selling must also take their part in the provision of an organization's new products if these products are to be a success.

Whilst I was teaching a group of MBA students, one of the course members who was employed in the health service said to me, 'Why are you always talking about the design of cars and other manufactured products, when nearly all of us are employed in the service sector?' This was fair criticism and my answer was not very helpful. I explained that not a great deal of research had been undertaken into the management of design. Pratically all the research had emanated from the manufacturing sector – there had been almost none of consequence undertaken into the management of the design of service products. I believed the same principles applied, but I wasn't sure. What did they think?

This started a new area for research which took several directions. Could the theories of product design management for manufactured products be applied to the service sector? What were the differences and how could these be resolved? Can service products be designed? Well, they can, and this book shows how they can – effectively and efficiently.

The research for this book took the form of looking at service product design and its management, where ideas come from, the steps they went through and who was involved in the various stages of design. The data was collected from approximately 160 organizations over a period of two years.

The most common cause of service product failure is the same as for any other product – poor market research. Organizations do not find out what their customers want and, therefore, do not fulfil their potential customers' needs better than their competition. Another common deficiency found in service product design is the inadequacy of specifications. One finding of the research was that there needs to be several distinct specifications that are focused on particular areas early in the design process and these are subsequently compiled into one complete (non-contradictory) Service Design Specification (SDS).

One aspect of service product design which is quite different from product design is the provision of a service product within an organization, such as the installation of a new computer system or a telephone exchange. The procedures described in this book will work for these intra-organizational activities as well as for the provision of a service product to an outside market.

At the same time that I was researching service design, my wife, Gillian, was conducting research into the way people behave and communicate in organizations. Included in this work was research into the people side of the management of design, the structure and operation of design teams and their training. As this work is complementary to the work on service product design, we have been able to combine our findings in compiling this book. We are thus able to show not only what should be done and when it should be done, but also how it should be done and who should do it.

Who this book is for

The first two-thirds of this book is for practitioners new to the subject of Total Service Design and also for students studying the subject of Innovation and Design Management on management courses (MBA, DMS, BTEC, HND and other business degrees). It is also aimed at those people who make up or co-ordinate multidisciplinary design teams. This will include the company directors through the echelons of the organization to those who are responsible for implementing the decisions taken. All involved should understand the design process and their place in it.

The final third of the book is directed at those who will actually be designing service products in organizations. In this part the early stages of the process or 'front end of design', where mistakes are most commonly made, are described in greater detail.

The Management of Innovation and Design is becoming an increasingly important subject on both undergraduate and postgraduate management courses. Of these postgraduate courses, the following has been said about the subject in a joint report by the CNAA, DTI and Design Council (1984):

> In order to improve the competitive position of UK companies, managing design should be included in postgraduate courses (MBA, MSc, DMS, Postgraduate Diploma and others). Ideally, 10 per cent of time should be devoted to the subject and at least 5 per cent is necessary to cover the basic topics. The aim should be for the same amount of coverage as 'traditional core subjects'.

Most of these postgraduate management courses are part-time and the majority of those people taking these courses are employed in the service sector. This book has been written as a course book for these people.

Furthermore, if you are considering starting your own small business from the product/service viewpoint you will find that this book will work for you. The sequence to be followed is the same and the emphasis is the same, although the other aspects of starting a company, e.g. taxes, grants, etc., are not considered.

Napoleon and Oliver Cromwell made two similar statements. The former said that the man who knows exactly where he is going doesn't go very far, whereas the latter said that a person who doesn't know where he's going goes a long way. Unfortunately the process of Total Design cannot indicate the final outcome at the beginning or the exact route to get there. What this process can do is show who should be following this approximate route and the pitfalls they are likely to meet along the way.

═ Service product design and small business start-ups ═

The failure rate of new products and service products is high, but often when a product fails the organization has others to fall back on and so will survive. Small service businesses are often one-product companies set up to provide one particular type of service using a limited range of skills. This means that the failure of a service product often causes the failure of the business. More than fifty per cent of new small businesses fail within the first five years.

The procedures described in this book will work for many aspects of starting a new business. I discovered this by accident when asked to lecture on small business courses. Whilst investigating the area for the seminars I found that many of the *major* problems and pitfalls for the entrepreneur starting a small business were exactly the same as for anyone designing a new product or service. A small business consists of five people or less. Many people drift into business with plenty of enthusiasm, hard work and little cash but also with little direction. Their knowledge of their proposed market is often sketchy and certainly under-researched. When the series of seminars started I would question these new business people about their customers and competitors. It was a cruel truth that the majority had little idea of their market even though several had already invested in some capital equipment. I was able to show that they had not done the groundwork and would almost certainly fail.

This groundwork is relatively quick and inexpensive and parallels the recommendations outlined in this book.

The worked example of the design process shown at the end of this book uses a small business start up as an example.

What is a service?

There is not a clear distinction between manufactured products and service products. Although some companies are classified as being in the manufacturing sector and others in the service sector there is not as clear a cut off point as these classifications suggest but more of a continuum. All manufacturing organizations have a service element in them. A manufacturing company may also be involved in selling their product. Similarly, in the manufacturing plant itself there may be a canteen, fire service, or telephone exchange. Also most service organizations will have an element of manufacture or production in them. This could include cooking food in a restaurant or the actual cutting of clients' hair in a hairdressers.

Services have been defined by the American Marketing Association as: 'Activities, benefits or satisfactions which are offered for sale, or provided in connection with the sale of goods.' This is not a recent definition and there have been several attempts to refine it.

Another good definition has been provided by Kotler (1986):

A service is any activity or benefit that one party can give to another that is essentially intangible and does not result in the ownership of anything. Its production may or may not be tied to a physical product.

Therefore, in its simplest form, a service is an intangible product. Often it cannot be stored. If it is not used during any period of time, its benefit is lost to both the customer and the organization selling it. Levitt (1981) said of this feature of a service that: 'The most important thing about intangibles is that customers usually don't know what they're getting until they don't get it.'

As an example of this intangibility of a service, consider a seat on a train or a room in a hotel. If left vacant the revenue that can be obtained for it on that day is lost. On the other hand, manufactured products can be stored (albeit with depreciation) to be sold another day. A car left in the showroom today can be sold tomorrow. Not so with most services.

However, the depreciation of most products which are stored is a lot higher than generally realized. The cost of actual storage, corrosion, protection, insurance, taxation, etc., can cost upwards of 20 per cent per annum with most metal goods, and the depreciation of some products is such that they could almost be treated as a service product. Bread, for example, if not sold today must be thrown away tomorrow. It has been estimated that one fifth of the bread purchased by London's hotels is thrown away. The realization in industry of the true cost of holding stocks has resulted in the reduction in stock holding through techniques such as 'Just-in-Time' (JIT). Industry is trying to operate more like the service sector by considering their products as intangible and only manufacturing them as they are required.

Service products are different in other respects. They are more likely to be available in many locations and usually command much higher profit margins. Generally, there is more customer contact and the customers' experience is almost as important as the treatment they receive. An example of this is private health care. The difference in technology and actual medication is no better and, perhaps, is inferior to that available in the NHS but the difference that makes people buy medical insurance is the *service* they receive – the speed of implementation, their comfort in hospital, better food, more time to talk with their medical advisor.

The difference between a successful and an unsuccessful service organization, then, is often the way in which customers are treated. In a hairdresser's shop it may be the way in which customers are welcomed – one's coat being taken and a cup of tea offered. A short wait, the attractiveness of the decor and the pleasant personality of the hairdresser will all influence the customer's impression of that establishment. All this must be designed into the service, which, in some ways, can make the design of a service product more complicated than that of a manufactured product. The 'people side' of design is more important in a service product and must be considered right at the start of the process in the specification.

The inability to store service products causes a major design difficulty. Avoiding bottlenecks that result in queueing at peak times, but also avoiding staff remaining idle at other times, is another important aspect in the design of a service product. Again, a hairdresser's is a good example. Most people apparently want their hair done on Friday afternoon and evening and during Saturday. Mondays, on the other hand, are very quiet. This means that staff must be available at a time when most of them would like their time off and may be under-utilized at some other times.

Why does a service product need to be designed?

A service product is very similar, in many respects, to a manufactured product. Levitt (1980) suggested that there is no such thing as a service company; only companies which have relatively higher service components than others. He stated that all companies could be placed on a single continuum with manufacturing and services simply being the two extremes. This would suggest that service products should be designed in similar manner to manufactured products.

Colin Clipson (1988), Professor of Architecture and Planning at the University of Michigan, says, 'It is important that we design not for just the product but the environment in which it is used . . . making everyday life more comfortable and more accessible and reassuring.' A service product must fulfil the needs of the customer, compete with the competition and be made available. In short, it has to be designed and this requires management. Until recently, by not realizing that a service product had to be designed, most were offered to the public in an inadequate state, having been put together in an inefficient manner. Roy Rothwell (1977) notes that 'responsibility for the success or failure of innovations rests with the innovating company's own management.' Mark Oakley (1984) confirms this by saying that design problems are generally not 'a lack of design skills, but an inability to manage design'.

Seventy per cent of the working population in Britain and the USA are now employed in the service sector and, therefore, the management process behind these products has taken on an increasing importance.

Hugh Davidson (1976), in his successful book on marketing, said that,

Competitive advantage is achieved whenever you do something better than competitors . . . having a better product is one of the most powerful competitive advantages, especially if the nature of the advantage is important to the customer.

This can only be achieved by understanding what customers want and then by giving it to them in a profitable manner, through well-managed design.

Chapter 2

Design management

What is design?

Christopher Lorenz (1983), Management Editor of *The Financial Times,* once said:

> I am delighted that we have managed to avoid any discussion about the definition of terms, because I think that is the way to get over a problem from which the design world is suffering severely at present; of people either making inflated claims about the subject or trying to dissect it with a sterile pair of intellectual tweezers.

Unfortunately, for those who are responsible for the design of products and services that have to meet the needs of customers, this 'dissecting' is essential. Unless everyone involved has a common understanding of design and, therefore, a common goal, design failure is the likely result.

Design is one of those words that seems to have a multitude of definitions. It means different things to different people: the way something looks, Computer Aided Design (CAD), or the way something performs. Walsh *et al.* (1988) state that 'the popular image of design is associated with fashion, style and a "colour supplement" lifestyle'. This image, they argue, is partly responsible for the fact that 'in many British firms design is not regarded as worthy of much time, effort and expense and designers tend to be regarded by managers with suspicion'. But design is crucial to all companies and design must be regarded as a total process.

The earliest definition that we have found that describes Total Design was by Morton (1976) who, though talking about innovation, described it as:

> A connected process in which many and sufficient creative acts, from research through service, couple together in an integrated way for a common goal.

We will be refining this later but it is essentially correct. Morton also describes the multidisciplinary nature of new product development.

Total Design is relatively new. In some respects some companies have undertaken Total Design for a lot longer, but many have kept the stages of the design process strictly separated. This mechanistic approach and lack of communication has resulted in badly designed, unsuccessful, products.

This book introduces the theory of Total Design to services, where the problem is probably not as bad but could still be much improved. Part of the reason lies with our education system in which people specialize when still quite young and continue to specialize throughout their subsequent education and training. Typically, at the age of fourteen, those good at 'arts' subjects are separated from those good at the 'sciences'. After taking their arts or science qualifications at school they go into quite different faculties at college or university, or take quite different vocational qualifications. As a result they do not get the opportunity to communicate about each other's different attitudes and opinions. The various 'factions' then meet at work and do not know how others think or operate. Management courses are one of the few areas where people from these different disciplines are given the opportunity to meet and talk.

Arthur Francis and Diane Winstanley (1989) state that: 'It is now accepted by most organizations that rigid demarcation between departments and a reliance on hierarchy to liaise is ineffective.' Total Design is a multidisciplinary process where all who can make an input must be involved. This is not as easy as it sounds, especially if there are a large number of people to be included, but is possible as will be shown.

Most definitions of Total Design tend to consider the process only up to the point where a product is manufactured or sold. Perhaps this is because observers fail to appreciate that there is much more still to be done. But design must be considered beyond this to include implementation, subsequent improvement and, we believe, 'disposal' as well. This may be more apparent with physical products. Consider the difficulties now being experienced in the disposal of Magnox nuclear power stations. These were designed for a life of twenty years which was later extended to thirty. In the design of these stations their 'disposal' was barely considered and it is now realized that it will take about a hundred years and cost £800 million to take down each Magnox reactor – and they are still not sure how they are going to do it. Covering them with concrete, painting them green, and calling them 'a hill' was one serious suggestion. This is an extreme example, but if you consider the disposal of your service and all the stages up to that disposal whilst you are assessing it right at the early stages, such disasters can be avoided.

We believe that ecological and 'green' issues will dominate thinking in the next ten years, and maybe beyond. As a result designers will have to focus more on energy and resource consumption in both the production and use of their designs.

Under the broad heading of 'disposal' can be included some other factors. Maintenance involves a great deal of planning and cost. Great savings are claimed for the introduction of 'Just-in-Time' (JIT) in manufacturing industry and one of the greatest areas of saving is in the elimination of stocks. If such savings are possible with just the stocks of work in progress and raw materials, what is the value tied up in the stocking of spare parts? If spares are to be provided they must be held in warm, dry, secure warehouses. These spare parts need to be protected against depreciation and theft, yet be accessible to those who need them. People must be trained in how to supply and fit these parts and service manuals will need to be written. Some parts will have to be held for up to twenty years. The cost of organizing a maintenance function is vast and this must be considered at an early stage of the design process. Perhaps you can plan to offer the servicing and maintenance contracts as another new product.

If the product is of the type where maintenance is likely to be required at some stage then this must also be designed to be effective. The importance of designing the maintenance function was brought into sharp relief whilst we were writing this book. The printer on our low-cost word processor stopped working. It was taken back to the shop and we were told that it would be returned to the makers and would, probably, take seven to ten days to be fixed. After many phone calls we eventually had the printer returned after thirteen weeks. The reason the makers gave was that all the spare parts are made abroad and none are stocked in this country. Therefore, any component that has failed is individually purchased from abroad and this is the typical time expected for delivery. You can imagine from this simple story how poor service and maintenance function design can certainly have an effect on follow-up sales.

The alternative is to make the design maintenance free, or 'disposable'. With manufactured products this tends to position the design in the low-cost sector of the market. Furthermore, the strength of a service-free product is the strength of the weakest component. There is little purpose in designing all but one of the parts to last twenty years if that one fails after six months. The life of such a product is the life of that weakest component. Designing a product to be maintenance-free is not an easy option but a difficult design problem and one to be considered very early in the design process.

Disposal of most things is becoming more difficult and companies are increasingly being held responsible world-wide for the dumping of products at the end of their life. Decisions should be taken, again at the start of the design process, on possible difficult disposal problems. This may mean that certain toxic and hazardous materials will be avoided in the design to be replaced by, perhaps, more expensive but more acceptable materials. This may cost more at the beginning but will be an overall saving over the total life of the product.

Perhaps the product may include items that it is worth reclaiming. This can lead to a whole additional new service being set up to reclaim and recycle these items. You could benefit from this aspect of design but only if you are actively seeking such opportunities. You should be planning for this aspect, again, early in the design process.

All these additional factors would only have been considered if your organization was committed to Total Design.

As design is such a diverse process it must include a lot of people from different areas of the organization with various skills. All of these people who can make an input must be involved if all the necessary factors to be included are to be given sufficient attention. This can include a large number of people all of whom will need to make a contribution to the total process. As a result the people side of design is a complicated design problem in itself.

Clearly, as service design is such a complicated process it will be necessary to backtrack to check or update as circumstances or the market changes. Therefore, design is *iterative*. We cannot over-emphasize the importance of iteration. Although we take a top-to-bottom approach in describing the design process it will never be possible to go through all the stages without repeating, checking and updating aspects which have gone before. This is because new information becomes available and also, during the time that the service is being designed, markets alter. Where possible, the service that is put on to the market will reflect the most up-to-date needs of that market. Keep backtracking and incorporating the changes as they occur. This is difficult but necessary. Iteration itself can be a problem as this must be controlled otherwise one will never reach a final acceptable solution.

Professor Joe Black (1989), formerly of Bath University, described the 'seven C's of successful design'. These are:

Customer
Competition
Costs
Concept
Compromise
Construction and
Communication.

These require a co-ordinating structure and all are included in this book.

Total Service Design can now be defined: it is a multidisciplinary, iterative, process that takes an idea and/or market need forward to implementation or selling. Total design must include all aspects up to the point of product disposal. This definition is similar, in effect, to that for manufactured products but there are some significant differences *en route* as we shall discuss.

The differences and similarities between service design and product design

Essentially, there is far less difference between product design and service design than one would, at first glance, expect. There are many similarities in the stages of the process and in the area where management should direct its emphasis.

13

Sidney Gregory (1966), who was writing sensible things about design before many of us had thought of design as a total process, wrote in the mid-1960s: 'The process of design is the same whether it deals with the design of a new oil refinery, the construction of a cathedral or the writing of Dante's *Divine Comedy*.' He then goes on to describe an iterative open system of design decision-making which relates social and organizational objectives and constraints.

Although Gregory was right in most of what he wrote, his statement is not entirely correct. There are differences and these we shall describe throughout this book. For a first example, consider *service protection*.

With a new manufactured product or manufacturing process it is possible to protect the designs from being copied through patents or by registering the design. This is not possible with a service; as Voss (1985) states, copyrights don't exist to protect a service-based company. This makes the design of services even more difficult. The only way to survive with your new designs is to make them better suited to your potential customers' needs and keep them a secret until the service is ready to be put onto the market. If they are launched with a fair degree of publicity it may be possible to surprise your competitors and get a good lead in the market before they can catch up. An example of this would be a new type of mortgage from a building society.

Even with patented products generally the protection can be circumvented or improved upon, unless the innovators have avoided what Stuart Pugh (1981) calls 'concept vulnerability'. This can be achieved by optimizing the design at the concept stage, ensuring thoroughness at the embodiment stage, and employing a patent agent to write the application to cover a broad area of protection. This is not easy, is expensive and time consuming. Therefore, with most products it is wiser to get the product onto the market and continue designing the next model and build up the customer base before the competition have had time to react. Investigating other people's patent applications is a common way for competitors to discover a company's future products and market thrust. Patents are a mixed blessing which those designing services are, in some ways, fortunate to avoid.

The differences between services and manufactured products also highlight the resultant differences in the emphasis in design. In manufacturing the main resource tends to be materials which are converted into a tangible product. The customer is not usually involved in the production process. Therefore, the production of a good can be isolated from its consumption. However, a service is often produced and consumed simultaneously and involves the customer. With a service, labour is the main utilization and a 'capability' is the product being sold. As a result the important consideration for the location of a service is to be near potential customers. With manufactured products a location near raw materials, suppliers or transport may be of greater importance.

The responsiveness and flexibility of a service is often damaged if the service is in one large location, whereas in manufacturing a large plant can benefit from economies of scale and with automation flexibility may be low.

Services have been shown to be more profitable than manufactured products. In his study of 25 companies Blumberg (1989) found that the profit margin of services was 15 – 25 per cent before tax, while for products it was 7 – 11 per cent. The implications on return on investment was even more dramatic – for services it was 70 – 80 per cent. Therefore, Blumberg (1989) concluded that: 'Organizations are increasingly looking to their service function as a strategic source of revenue and competitive differentiation.'

There are other differences between manufactured product design and service product design and these will become apparent through the subsequent stages of this book.

Design models

Twiss (1987) argues that decisions will be better if they are made with an understanding of the processes at work and within a 'conceptual framework'. This conceptual framework is the Design Model.

A design model also shows the general direction of the design process. The following sequence for the design process was supplied by a student, copied from the council notice board where he worked.

Design process:

1. Enthusiasm.
2. Disillusionment.
3. Panic.
4. Search for the Guilty.
5. Punish the Innocent.
6. Praise the Non-participants.

Let's hope we can do better.

Academics spend a great deal of time discussing and disagreeing over the model that shows the various stages that are followed in total design. Most of these models have been compiled by engineers and thus have an engineering bias. We have looked at many from various researchers and the vast majority show similar core stages in the same sequence to the point where one would believe them to be axiomatic. This is shown in Fig. 2.1.

Cooper (1983) uses a model that has the sequence:

Idea – Preliminary Assessment – Concept – Development – Testing – Trial – Launch

with each stage evaluated by a go/kill/hold decision. This evaluation at the end of each stage of design seems to be popular with practitioners. These decision points tend to encourage those involved in the design process to focus

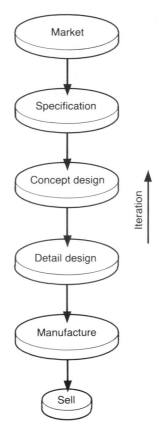

Fig. 2.1 Design core.
Courtesy of *Patent World* January 1990.

their attention on the main aims of that which is being designed.

We have said that, in our opinion, design ends with disposal, so most of these models end too soon. Furthermore, with certain products it is unlikely that they would be manufactured before they were sold, for example a battleship. Services throw this into sharp relief where the relative sequence in the process of the 'manufacturing' and 'selling' stages are often swopped over and in some products, such as computer software, they are often sold before the detail design is undertaken.

A design model is included in the British Standard *A Guide to Managing Product Design* (BS 7000) and is shown in Figs 2.2 and 2.3. It is a good model which at least takes the process as far as disposal. It does have some features, though, with which we are unhappy. Design is separated out as being only part of the process when, in fact, all the stages are part of Total Design. Furthermore, design for manufacture is shown to be a stage after detail design

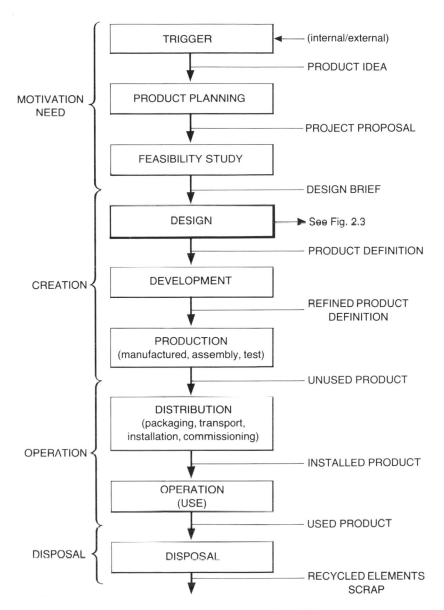

Fig. 2.2 A design model. (Extract from BS 7000: 1989. Reproduced with the permission of BSI.)

(*see* Fig. 2.3). These two stages must be undertaken together otherwise products can be designed that are difficult to make. Designing the product and designing the method of manufacture together is one of the reasons given for the speed and success that the Japanese have had with their product design. Generally,

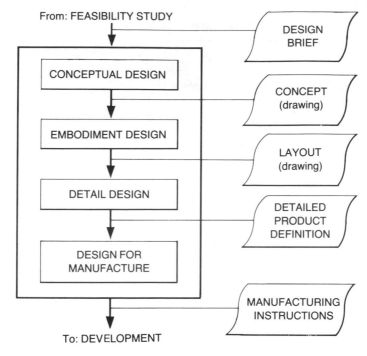

Fig. 2.3 A design model – detail. (Extract from BS 7000: 1989. Reproduced with the permission of BSI.)

design models should be treated with care and not followed in a dogmatic fashion.

In our research we have established one important fact: for successful service design the first three stages of the model must be followed in sequence, namely:

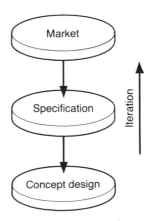

Fig. 2.4 The first three stages of the design core.

Fig. 2.5

Business environment	Layer 1	Main management guidelines Management commitment Quality and Reliability Reacting to market pull Effective sales unit Financial control Organizational control Timescales
Select the product champion Form design circle		
Overall business objectives	Layer 2	Objective Idea generating/trigger Strategic specification Initial marketing specification Budgetary requirements (required return and maximum costs)
Main design review (go/hold/abandon)		
Idea formulation, analysis and evaluation	Layer 3	Explanation, preliminary assessment Business analysis Market research/desk research Identify, qualify, quantify need Competition analysis Relevant innovations Initial costing
Layer 4	FEASIBILITY STUDY Main design review: Assessment and screening PRODUCT / SERVICE DEFINITION(S) (go/hold/abandon)	
Planning	Layer 5	Product status specification Find product status (macro and micro) Service audit
	Layer 6	Preliminary technical specification Costings refined, service model Preliminary marketing specification Compromise Expansion potential
	Layer 7	Assemble full service design specification
Main design review: Assessment (go/hold/abandon)		
Concept	Layer 8	Concept identification Concept assessment/evaluation Concept selection Costings refined
Main design review: (go/hold/abandon)		
Development	Layer 9	Embodiment design Full technical specification Dynamic product design Process status
	Layer 10	Static product design Dynamic process design Dynamic product testing
	Layer 11	Detail design Dynamic process testing Static process design Maintenance and Servicing facility design Main marketing strategy (promotion, pricing, distribution) Full cost of the design
Main design review: (go/hold/abandon)		
Implementation	Layer 12	The 'doing it' stage of the design Product prototype testing: trial, user test Manufacture/production/construction Purchase Set up operation
Main design review: (go/hold/abandon)		
Commercialization	Layer 13	Launch/announce/educate Full operation Sell Use
Monitoring		Assessment Evaluation (financial) Reaction Appraisal
		Update ──▶Re-design ───── FEEDBACK Update ──▶Re-design ───── Disposal

MAIN DESIGN FLOW

ITERATION

Fig. 2.5 Suggested framework for the design model.

19

The subsequent stages tend to vary depending on the type of service, but iteration is still important throughout the process.

The names used for these subsequent stages also vary. Some companies we found seemed happy to use 'detail design', 'manufacture', and 'sell', albeit in inverted commas, but these terms are not universally applicable or acceptable. 'Implementation' was one which was popular in our study to describe the 'manufacturing' stage. Therefore, there appears to be no one design model that satisfactorily describes service design.

We have also developed a design model (Fig. 2.5) that includes many of the stages that should be considered in the sequence shown. This can guide your planning for the design of services, but you should endeavour to develop a design model to suit your own particular service. We have provided a series of key steps and areas that warrant consideration. It is advisable to stick to the broad structure and additional stages should be added, rather than omit or bypass any of the stages given here.

Some of the terms used in the model will be unfamiliar at this stage but their meaning and implication will become clear as you progress through this book.

Product failure and where it occurs

When we talk about design nowadays it is often quite difficult to identify which services or products are successful and which are a failure. R. G. Cooper (1988), a well known analyst of new products, has written that 'an understanding of past failures yields important clues to what should be done differently in the future.' Some of the best designs, especially of buildings, would not have been classed as successful if today's criteria were applied to them. It is very unlikely that the Taj Mahal would have been built in today's industrial world. Some large projects, like the Channel Tunnel and Concorde, have been possible through a vast initial investment. Most of us will work for small organizations concerned with designing far less magnificent products and services. Those of us who do work in such organizations can only judge the success of a product or service by the profit it brings in to the organization.

Stating that a design is a technical or aesthetic success, is a flagship for the organization or has brought in a great deal of publicity and promotion when it has failed to make a profit is hiding from the truth. In business today, where the survival of an organization depends on the 'bottom line', the only real measure of success can be financial. A new product or service must make a profit in simple trading terms or it is a failure.

Certainly, if profit were the only criteria for success, this world would be a drab and poorer place without such beautiful buildings as the Taj Mahal. We live on the flight path of Concorde and still marvel over its beauty and power, but we are glad that we didn't have any money invested in its design.

If your organization is to get involved in such an enterprise ensure, first, that there is somebody out there who will pick up the bill.

Several writers have given a definition of design failure. Foxall (1984) defines it as 'a product failing to live up to its company expectations in the market' and O'Shaughnessy (1984) describes it as 'occurring whenever management regrets the new product introduction'. Both are good definitions but perhaps not sufficiently quantifiable to be generally usable.

Without financial success from design, for most organizations the results would be decline or extinction. The financial success of design is certainly less glamorous than other aspects, but it is the only one that will ensure continued employment. For this reason we suggest that you judge the success of a design by asking the question: 'Would you have liked your money invested in it?'

By this reckoning, Concorde would be judged a design failure – and it was. Nearly £2 billion was invested to end up with BA flying six and Air France five Concordes, with an annual working profit of about £20 million. The other measures of design success, in the face of such heavy financial failure, pale into insignificance.

The service you design can only be judged a success if it returns a profit for your organization, and the greater the profit, over a specified period of time, in relation to the amount initially invested the more successful the design can be considered to be.

By this measure the majority of designs are failures. Figure 2.6 shows, typically, where in the design process of manufactured products these failures occur. The contents of this figure we determined from the findings of various researchers. It shows, not unexpectedly, a high failure rate at the start of the design process, which reduces the further one proceeds through it.

These and other researchers have also identified the causes of design failure. The overall reason for failure from many studies has been clearly stated by Cooper (1988): 'The overwhelming cause of failure is due to companies not understanding the customer's requirements.' This cause did not alter in the twenty years over which Cooper analysed results.

Twiss (1987) observed: 'There is substantial evidence from both sides of the Atlantic that a market orientation is still woefully absent in many decisions and that is a major source of failure.' Conversely, Project SAPPHO (Rothwell, 1972) came up with the following main factor underlying success: 'understanding of user needs'.

When one realizes that finding out what the customer requires is determined through market research and that market research should be conducted very early in the design process, the situation that exists in many organizations looks gloomy. These failures result from organizations not having done any or having carried out inadequate market research. Therefore, most organizations are taking an inadequately market researched product idea right through the design process, only to realize that not enough people want it when it goes on sale. This is too late and a frightening waste of money, time and resources.

21

Look again at Fig. 2.6. The fact that most products fail at the start of design is not usually a problem. An organization will consider many ideas and abandon most of these early in the process. These are design failures but good design management. It is important that an organization should appraise a large number of potential new products and a healthy sign that most are abandoned at this stage.

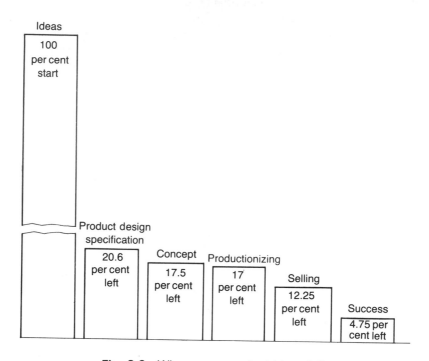

Fig. 2.6 Where new product ideas fail.

The problem occurs at the other end of the design process. Typically, for every three products that are put on to the market, only one is a success. Two have been taken through the entire design process and have had a large amount of money invested in them, only to fail when being offered to the customers. These failures have a lot to do with inadequate market research and are a definite sign of bad design management. Of course, market failure is not the only cause of new product failure. Other reasons for failure can be described as technical failure, financial, badly organized selling, the product being too late or superseded, or, with large products, political causes.

Design is expensive and requires financial control. A financial commitment in the form of a specific budget must be given right at the start of the design process. Although it is difficult to anticipate the cost of a design, especially if innovation is involved, it must still be attempted. Figure 2.11 in the next section can help in this respect as it can be used to subdivide the cost of each stage of the design process into their component parts. This can allow the budget to be allocated and give an early warning of costs spiralling out of control.

Technical failure is mainly due to errors occurring at the detailing or implementation stage, quite late in the design process. With manufactured goods technical failure can often result in some quite spectacular catastrophes. Examples are the 'unsinkable' *Titanic* that sank when it hit an iceberg because the bulkheads had not been designed high enough to prevent water flowing over the top of them, and the Tacuma Narrows Bridge ('Galloping Gertie') that literally shook itself to pieces because the designers did not allow for the effect of crosswind on the natural frequency of the structure. There are many examples but the most common manifestation of this in a product or service is that it just doesn't work properly.

Ineffective and inefficient selling is a fault in the organization and often not a problem with the actual product or service at all. But selling is part of Total Design and potential customers must be aware that services are available and they must be able to obtain them. Plan the promotion and distribution of the service early in the design process. After market research the customer profile should be apparent. It is simply then a case of informing those identified, then providing the service through the most effective promotion and distribution systems to reach them.

Distribution may take the form of the site location, mail order, sales personnel and various other methods of selling. Promotion may be through advertising, press releases, exhibitions, sponsorship and other marketing techniques. In most books on marketing these are described under the heading of two of the 'four P's' – place and promotion. The other two P's of the marketing mix are price and product.

Political failures are often outside the control of many organizations. Failures occurring due to changes in government policy may be unexpected but, in general, there is sufficient time to take remedial action. One case in which such action was not – and perhaps could not have been – taken was in the design of the M25 orbital motorway. The original plan called for four lanes in each direction. This was not accepted by the government and the result is a three lane highway that for too many hours each day is a 125 mile long car park. The extra lane would not have avoided jams but would have meant that traffic was moving freely for more hours of the day. The M25 is an unusual example as its very success is the cause of its failure.

Legislation allowing other companies (notably Mercury) to provide a telephone service, as well as allowing these companies to use BT's telephone lines, did not result in failure but did reduce BT's revenue. The legislation allowing the privatization of ancillary services in local government and the Health Service has caused the failure of these operations in some areas. Politics and its effects are one of the elements requiring consideration in the Service Design Specification which is written early in the design process. Endeavour

23

to identify potential political changes and be fully conversant with the state of government thinking.

Whatever the length of the mature phase of the product lifecycle, eventually the product will go into decline, usually having been superseded by a newer design (*see* Fig. 6.3). Hopefully, the organizations that designed the original will have made money from it and designed the product to replace the older version. The older product is now a failure but this need not mean a financial loss to the organization concerned. Having identified that decline is inevitable, further investment in the existing design should be stopped. One example of this with a manufactured product was in a company that made a particular component for military vehicles. A new (patented) design emerged from the competition which meant that decline for the original design was inevitable. Being aware of their demise in this particular product area the company set about maximizing profit. They stopped all development of the product as well as any further investment on manufacturing equipment. Through effective market research they knew that the product had only a limited and reducing life on the market, but they made a significant amount of revenue during this product's decline.

The organizations that are likely to suffer financially are those that endeavour to enter a market too late, just as the product, in that particular design configuration, is about to decline. Another cause of failure arises when organizations try to enter an established market during the mature part of the product lifecycle. If a market has become established with a particular design, then it is unwise to attempt market entry with another new design unless it is significantly better. An example here is the Philips Video 2000 video recorder which was introduced onto a market already dominated by the VHS system developed by JVC. The advantages of the Video 2000 were insufficient to shift existing users away from the familiar format.

The important feature to note, with almost all product failures, is that the likelihood of failure, in the overwhelming number of cases, should have been identified earlier, in most cases right near the start of the design process. Quite often it is poor design management that has resulted in products and services being taken through to implementation only for it then to become apparent that they will not be a success. This is the major claim for promoting greater management awareness at the early stages of the design process.

The cost of the various stages of design

We have shown where products tend to fail during the design process. We now consider the cost of the various stages of the process.

Figure 2.7 shows a curve originally identified by Buggie in 1961 and a similar curve is shown in BS 7000 *Guide to Managing Product Design*. This shows

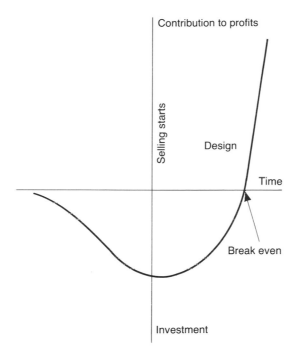

Fig. 2.7 The effect of investing in design.

that an initial investment is made and after a period of time the design is completed and the product is placed on the market. *If* the product is successful and sells well, there will still be a period of time before the breakeven point is reached, which may be some years. The initial investment will then have been clawed back. The product then goes into profit.

This is an over-simplification because the investment necessary for the design of new products and services usually has to be borrowed. Occasionally it can be financed from existing funds, but this is less usual. This means that, with an initial investment, there is the additional factor of the interest to be paid on borrowed money or the loss in revenue on existing funds not being left 'in the bank'. Therefore, the product must sell successfully for even longer to make up for this loss of interest. This is shown in Fig. 2.8.

But, as we have already shown, two out of every three products put on the market are failures and do not bring in any profit. Figure 2.9 shows a typical situation with two out of three failed products. 'X' is the loss and to this must be added the additional loss incurred paying the interest rate for the number of years that the design process has been continuing.

So for each product success the profit must not only cover the cost of designing that product but, typically, the other two products that are failures – including the additional cost of money. At the end of this, the organization

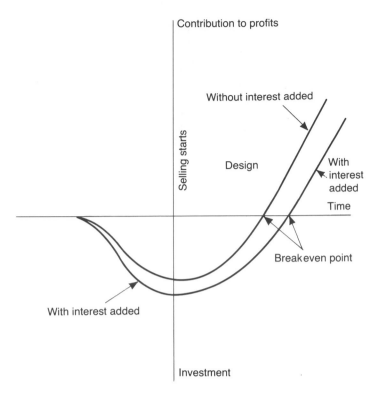

Fig. 2.8 The effect of interest.

and the shareholders expect a satisfactory return on their investment – more than they would get just by leaving their money in the bank or investing it elsewhere. This is shown in Fig. 2.10.

The picture has been made even more depressing by the author Starr (1963), who stated that the waste lay not only in the costs of designing failures, but also in the lost opportunity of spending the time more profitably on designing something else.

An organization must continuously design new products or services if it is not to stagnate and die. But the cost of designing failures can cause an organization to cease to exist far faster than if it undertook no design at all. Such is the importance of correctly managing new products and services.

We have taken the cost of the various stages of design from our research and the research of others. This is shown in Fig. 2.11. The products that were used in the compilation of this figure were mainly manufactured products or fast-moving consumer goods. Costs rise dramatically the further a new product design proceeds through the process, with almost half the costs being incurred at the preparation for manufacturing stage.

There has been no published research, as yet, that describes the cost of

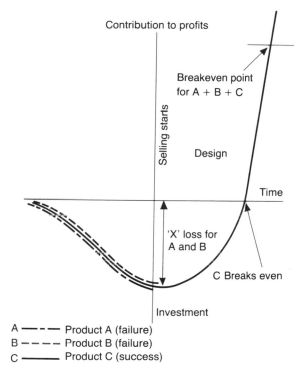

Fig. 2.9 The effect of failed products.

the various stages of service design. We have started to compile information in this area. The main difficulty in costing the overall sequence for all services is the variation in what comprises the implementation stage. The 'doing it' stage may be high as when refitting a shop or purchasing a computer system, or relatively low as when starting a consultancy or firm of window cleaners. What we have found is that with services the rise in costs in the later stages are not as pronounced as with manufactured products. But even with services the majority of investment is required during these later stages.

Sunk costs

The theory behind sunk costs is very simple but in practice it can be quite difficult to carry out. Suppose that a company has embarked upon a design project. After a period of time and large financial investment they find that, for whatever reason, the market for this service has greatly reduced. The question is, should they abandon the project?

Consider the design project shown in Fig. 2.12. Already £900,000 has been

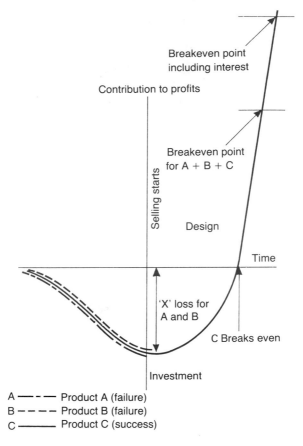

Fig. 2.10 The effect of failed products plus interest.

spent on it but the latest estimation for the anticipated market is only £200,000. The product will be a financial failure to the company and it is not yet fully designed and ready for the market. Should the product be abandoned immediately or should the design work be completed and the product put onto the market?

With sunk costs what has been spent is lost. There is little point in trying to apportion blame except to find out what went wrong to avoid the same mistakes occurring again. The main concern is whether to finish the design. An estimation must be made of the cost of completing the design project. Certainly if the cost of the remaining development exceeds more than £200,000 losses will further increase and further work should immediately cease. If the cost is less than £200,000 it would appear that it is worthwhile continuing as there would be a profit on the remaining investment.

The decision is not that easy. First of all the cost of borrowing the money

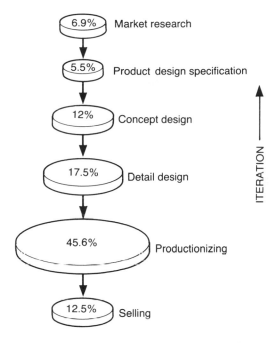

6.9% Market research

5.5% Product design specification

12% Concept design

17.5% Detail design

45.6% Productionizing

12.5% Selling

ITERATION

Fig. 2.11 The cost of new product design.

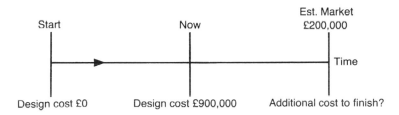

Start

Now

Est. Market
£200,000

Time

Design cost £0

Design cost £900,000

Additional cost to finish?

Fig. 2.12 The effect of sunk costs.

to complete the project must be included in the sum. If the money to do the design is not being borrowed then the loss of interest for the money being invested must be considered. Furthermore, the lost opportunity must be appraised. It is difficult to put this into financial terms but some attempt must be made to anticipate the return that might be possible if the people and finance were directed towards another project.

Often it is a waste of resources to continue with one design and it would be better for the organization to embark on another. The cost to complete the project in this example would need to be quite a bit less than £200,000 to make continuance worthwhile.

In practice it is far more difficult to abandon a design project in this situation than it would first appear. Most of the money has been spent and there is a fair degree of commitment to the project. People are bound to lose face (and perhaps their jobs as well). And no one can be certain that the market does no longer exist. More usually a company will cut down on some of the design expenditure and give the project a lower priority. This has the effect of lowering morale and causing the service to be late on the market, which can make the situation even worse regarding potential sales. The service is then left on the market for a period in the hope that it might 'take off' – rarely it does. Gradually the realization comes that the design is yet another failure and it can be quietly removed from the market. Those responsible, by then, will be fully involved in another product and will not feel the 'pain' of the failure so intensely. The damage to the organization, though, will be worse than if the design had been abandoned much earlier.

It takes strong management to take a firm decision part way through the design process to abandon a product or service. This decision becomes more difficult the further the project has progressed through the process.

══════ **Where you should direct your emphasis** ══════

From the preceding sections of this chapter, it can be seen that the early stages, or 'front end of design', is the low-cost end of the design process. It is also the part of design where the main management decisions are taken.

Once a design has reached beyond the specification stage it is, usually, possible to think of some concept that will fulfil it. Having done this, it is, usually, possible to provide detailed drawings and to implement and sell the product. Therefore, if the decision hasn't been taken to abandon the design before it gets beyond the specification stage then it is more than likely that a product will appear on the market. Looking at the results of product development, mainly of fast-moving consumer goods, typically 70 per cent of new product ideas that reach the concept stage of the design process eventually are put on the market. These stages are almost mechanical – turn the handle and a result will appear.

The seniority of those involved tends to reduce the further one gets through the process, even though the costs rise dramatically. But then, having spent all this money, many such products are market failures. This means that, unless a decision has been taken to abandon a product early in the design process, then it is quite likely that the subsequent stages of the design process will be completed.

Therefore, management must concentrate their efforts early in the process to identify potential failures and eliminate them. In Total Design, design managers will be making the most important decisions at a stage where, in the traditional structure of product design, they were not yet involved.

This 'front-end loading' will increase the time and, therefore, the cost of these early stages quite considerably. But suppose you doubled the time for the first two stages of the design process (or doubled the manpower involved and kept the time taken as before). Typically, this would only increase the total cost of the design process by about 13 per cent. The breakdown of the stages of the design of manufactured products would then be as shown on Fig. 2.13.

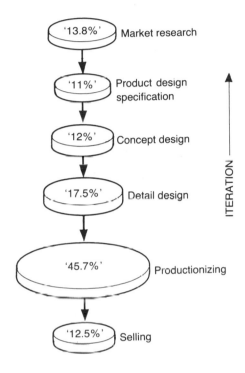

Fig. 2.13 The effect of increasing spending on the early stages of new product design. Of every £100 originally spent double that spent on the first two stages. This will increase the total cost of design by 12.4 per cent but reduce the prospect of failure.

As stated in the previous section, an ideal breakdown of the costs for the various stages of the design of services does not yet exist. But although there are no hard and fast rules, if you are spending less than 50 per cent on the early stages (as shown in Fig. 2.14) then perhaps you should reassess how you are designing services.

The net effect would be to increase greatly the chances of identifying potential failures through better market research and a more thorough specification. The designs still in the system would then have a greater potential for success. It could also mean that there will be time for more potential new product ideas to be assessed and the unfavourable ones abandoned early in

31

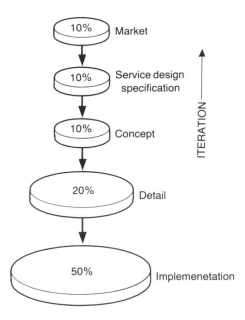

Fig. 2.14 A suggested breakdown in costs for the design of a service.

the design process. The current situation and the situation that should be aimed at is shown in Fig. 2.15.

Hopefully, with the majority of potential design failures removed from the system early on, those remaining will be a success. This is the ideal, and it is unlikely that such a perfect situation will be achieved – but it is a direction worth pursuing. With the current failure rate of two-thirds of all products put on sale there does not have to be a great improvement to give your organization a real competitive advantage.

If the failure rate can be reduced to 1 in 2 of products put on the market (and 50 per cent failure rate can hardly be considered good) then the cost of running the design function will be reduced by something approaching 30 per cent.

Those involved in the later stages of the process will have more confidence in the designs emerging from the earlier stages. They will know that there is less chance that they are wasting their time on unresearched, poorly specified products.

The obvious question here is that as this is so simple why doesn't every organization do it? The answer to this is partly because few organizations have truly costed out the various stages of their design process and that the separation of the various departments involved in design has helped to 'hide' the true situation. These barriers should now be broken down through Total Design. But probably the main reason has been that, in many organizations, the design process actually starts at the concept stage with assumptions, rather than

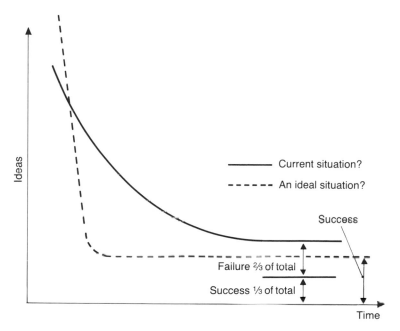

Fig. 2.15 New product elimination.

research, being made in the earlier stages of the design process.

By increasing the time spent or investment on the low-cost early stages of design the entire organization will become more effective in its new product development process. This raises the interesting prospect that 'fringe' product ideas will now become profitable as they no longer have to carry the burden of their own development costs, plus (typically) the costs of the two failures that usually accompany each success. They now need only carry one other to make the organization profitable. The corollary of this is that innovations, which hitherto it may have been necessary to avoid because the company couldn't risk any failures, (innovation being more risky) can now be considered. And all of this from an increase of, approximately, 13 per cent in costs at the front end of design.

════════ Abandoning a design ════════

Having said that the majority of new product ideas should be abandoned early in the design process, there needs to be a 'mechanism' to show how this should be done. Some people have stated that we over-emphasize abandoning a design project. But we stick with our belief that the quicker one can identify potential design failures, stop work on them and start on something more viable, the better.

Cooper (1983), who has investigated factors that lead to a successful design, says that there should be plenty of 'bail out' points. The deciding factor in the continuation of a project is whether it satisfies, at each stage, the subspecification. Therefore, at the end of each stage of the design process a review meeting will be held and a decision taken to proceed with the design. If the subspecification cannot be satisfied the project will not be immediately abandoned, but iterated back through the process to see if corrections can be made or the subspecification modified. Perhaps, the market requirements can be modified after further market research or a different selling medium selected, and so on. If corrections to the design or sufficient modifications to the subspecification are not possible, then the design will be abandoned.

The decision to abandon the project is the responsibility of the product champion and the only point where any design is abandoned should be at the *screening stage*. All designs that do not meet the specification should be iterated back to the product screening before it can be certain that a design is a failure. This iteration should not take more than a couple of days for almost all service designs.

<hr>

Summary

- If a design failure is to be avoided, everyone involved in the design process must have a common understanding and a common goal.

- Total Design is a multidisciplinary, iterative process which does not end when the product is sold to the customer. It continues beyond the implementation and through improvement stages, and must include consideration of the final disposal of the product.

- The least damage to a company is caused if potential failures are identified and abandoned early. With an effective system for design, which includes identifying failures and abandoning them at the early, low-cost stage in the design process, more new product ideas can be considered.

- Money spent must be viewed as sunk costs and the main decision that should be taken is whether the anticipated return, when the product is sold, exceeds the completion costs. If it doesn't then abandon it. Such decisions can usually be avoided if the early design stages have been properly completed.

The stages of
service design

Chapter 3

Marketing research

Introduction

'Time spent on reconnaissance is rarely wasted.'
(Field-Marshal Montgomery)

In many organizations the marketing research function is poorly undertaken and sometimes it is left to the sales manager to decide what information is required for the design of a product. In this section we briefly describe some aspects of marketing research which may improve the information that you can collect. This stage should be carried out before you have attempted to offer the service for sale to the public.

Marketing research is defined by the Institute of Marketing as the 'systematic and objective search for, and analysis of, information relevant to the identification and solution of any problem in the field of marketing'. It is about epistemology – or knowledge of the world – and brings into consideration the mix of qualities and price that will attract customers to your organization's products rather than those of the competition.

As Urban *et al.* (1987) say: 'Early in the design process the emphasis is on gaining an understanding of the consumer.' Marketing research is more extensive than market research, which only considers analysis of the size and nature of a particular market. Effective marketing research is vital but Catlin, quoted in Lovelock (1984), is cautious, however, in stating that research 'is not going to reveal some panacea . . . (it will just) give you some greater insights and some greater understanding.' We consider the most useful book covering this area is *The Marketing Research Process* by Margaret Crimp (1990).

Wilson (1972) identifies typical marketing research objectives as including establishing 'marketing characteristics and customer needs, desirable service features, attitudes, (and) marketing service costs.'

Marketing research covers:

1.   The *description* of channels through which products and services reach

customers, the way these products and services are used, and the perception and attitudes that lead to customer choice.

2.   The *explanation* of these attitudes, perceptions and behaviour.
3.   *Evaluation,* in which the cost-effectiveness of marketing designs are assessed.
4.   *Prediction,* in which trends and a proposed direction for action for future plans are specified.

When planning your marketing research we propose that you follow this sequence:

1.   Decide what your problem is.
2.   Set preliminary research objectives.
3.   Carry out exploratory research.
4.   Revise research objectives.
5.   Design the research method.
6.   Undertake a pilot survey.
7.   Estimate the time taken and the cost to obtain the data.
8.   Survey the data collection.
9.   Analyse and present findings.
10. Make marketing decisions.

Primary and secondary data

Marketing research can be divided into two broad categories: *secondary* data collection, which includes desk research, the collection of existing documentation and expert estimation; *primary* data collection, which includes interviewing, observation and experimentation.

Secondary data collection should always be undertaken first. Carry out some exploratory research but keep revising the research objectives in the light of the results and information obtained. Such collection is the principal source of marketing information. It is inexpensive and gathered quickly. A person with well-focused objectives can usually gain all the necessary information regarding a product in, typically, one full week's work.

Desk research is particularly important if you are considering export markets. It is far quicker and cheaper to find out local differences in legislation, customs, distribution methods, etc., from the UK than after arriving on foreign soil. There are several government and independent agencies that can help in these areas such as THE (Technical Help for Exporters). This research must study information available within the organization as well as that from outside. An organization will have records on sales, customers, production output and capacity, material usages and purchases, how and where products are distributed and promotion, as well as details of the cost of these. The amount of data available is generally far more than you need, though it can often be out of date or not relevant. Try to retain only useable information in your organization.

Most organizations are full of 'experts' who can provide you with estimates. For example, the sales personnel will have a knowledge of what they sell and to whom, where they sell it and how it is delivered. They will also know where they fail to sell and why, who their competitors are and in what ways the competitors are better or worse than their organization. Each department will have experts, who can provide 'free' information or data, which should be gleaned before seeking outside advice. Outside the organization it is possible to obtain information often at almost no cost, covering many aspects of products or organizations. Some examples are local libraries, *Kelly's*, *Yellow Pages*, *Who Owns Whom*, government statistics, census figures, etc.

One of the easiest and yet most effective methods of competition analysis is simply to list the advantages and disadvantages of any proposed new service with what is already on the market. For a new product to be a success it will need to be better than what already exists – being just as good isn't good enough. Primarily, listing these advantages and disadvantages will show if your new service will have a chance to succeed against the competition, but it will also show up some other things. It will demonstrate if you have correctly pinpointed your competitors and, therefore, your potential customers. Theodore Levitt (1981) of the Harvard Business School referred to the importance of understanding customers when he said that an organization 'must learn to think of itself not as producing goods or services but as buying customers, as doing the things that will make people want to do business with them'.

This listing will also show at which market niche you should be directing your service or where you need to do more market research. Furthermore, it will show the areas where you need to improve the proposed service. If a competitor has an advantage in certain areas, can these be incorporated into your design?

This type of competition analysis need only take a group of people two to three hours but can save quite a bit of work in the later stages and indicate the areas where subsequent design effort should be directed. It will also indicate whether the idea is unlikely to succeed and should be abandoned at this early stage before hardly any costs have been incurred.

To aid with this process a checklist of advantages and disadvantages (taken partly from Courtis (1988)) has been listed in Table 3.1. The list is obviously not exhaustive. Note that an advantage in one situation may be a disadvantage in another, for example, customers may want a 'fast time to complete' in a delivery service, but look upon it as a disadvantage in a fairground ride.

Table 3.1 Advantages or disadvantages of one design over another

1. Greater quality and reliability.
2. Demonstrably safer.
3. Easier maintenance.
4. Easier to use (ergonomics).
5. Lower price.
6. Better value.
7. Stronger (more robust, longer lasting).
8. Training easier.
9. Contract out — other organizations can make product or perform service, saving on overheads.

(1 — 9 are of greatest importance but relative importance may vary depending on the type of product and market.)

10. Performance:
    (a) More accurate.
    (b) Faster time to complete/less delay.
    (c) More range.
    (d) Higher load.
    (e) Quieter.
    (f) More economical:
        — Lower running costs.
        — Lower energy use.
        — Less effort.
    (g) Less pollution.
    (h) More 'add on' useful features.
    (i) Wider environmental use (or better protection from the environment).
    (j) Less interference.
    (k) Longer shelf life.
    (l) Longer life in use (or corrosion resistance).
    (m) More versatile.
    (n) More dedicated.

11. Physical:
    (a) Smaller/larger.
    (b) Lighter.
    (c) More convenient (parking, storage).
    (d) Easier to install.
    (e) Easier to obtain.

12. Aesthetics:
    (a) Better appearance.
    (b) Better finish.
    (c) More comfortable.
    (d) Better atmosphere.
    (e) More supportive.
    (f) Higher status:
        — Esteem.

- Fashion.
- Image.
- Prestigious.

13. Environment:
  (a) Less/easier legislation.
  (b) Less tax, insurance, etc.
  (c) Less anxiety.
  (d) More pleasant interpersonal relations.
  (e) More authoritative.
  (f) More enjoyable.
  (g) Guaranteed.
  (h) Recommended.
  (i) Market leader.
14. Personal:
  (a) Knowledgeable.
  (b) More honest.
  (c) More personal.
  (d) More trustworthy.
  (e) Less hurried.
  (f) Relaxed.
  (g) Direct.
  (h) Attentive.
  (i) Considerate.
  (j) Cheerful.
  (k) Punctual.
  (l) Professional.
  (m) Reassuring.
  (n) Chatty.
  (o) Respectful.
  (p) Quiet.
  (q) Competent.
  (r) Friendly.
  (s) Mature.
  (t) Young.
  (u) Direct.
15. Or just unique or different.

Figure 3.1 provides an example of a proposed new method of delivery service by courier in comparison with, perhaps, an existing service. Clearly the delivery service would benefit from offering both of these types of service.

The two services are complementary. The OAP service is less expensive, the motor cycle service is usually faster and can follow routes not served by bus.

This system of marketing research is, essentially, crude and if a product is not eliminated at this point, it will then be subjected to other more sophisticated, and time-consuming appraisals, such as parametric analysis.

Service offered: To deliver a parcel, weighing 1 kg, in 4 hours over a distance of 8 miles, in London.

Existing service: Delivery by motor cycle courier.

New service: OAPs travelling by bus, using a bus pass.

Advantages of new service	Disadvantages of new service
Low pay	Smaller operating range
Casual labour	Slower
Can use bus pass	Can only work where free bus pass available
Less overheads (National Insurance) therefore, cheaper	Cannot operate during rush hour
No union problems	Limited carrying capacity (2 kg)
Less affected by travel hold-ups (bus or tube or walk)	Can only operate when public services are operating
Quieter	Cannot be reached as easily by radio (e.g. when on train)
Safer/less insurance cover	Less fit
Less affected by maintenance problems	Less reliable (illness/casual labour)
May know area better	
Smarter/better image	
No pollution	
No parking problems	
No driving licence/skill needed	
Less chance of motoring offences (parking, speeding, accidents)	
More mature	
More respectful (?)	

Fig. 3.1 Appraisal of new courier delivery service.

Parametric analysis

Parametric analysis is another inexpensive form of desk research which is a useful tool for marketing and design that can be used to identify a product's place in the market when compared to the competition. It will show which products are leading the market and where the popular areas of design are clustered. Once, through using parametric analysis, we identified a potentially dangerous design, which was initially observed as being at the 'risky' extreme of the parametric plot, well away from the other manufacturers. The company was informed and took action.

Parametric analysis can be used to identify the areas of strength and weakness as part of competition analysis at the start of the design process. It can also be used at the other end of design to appraise your service against the competition, especially when you are updating a service.

Parametric analysis takes two major forms. In one, various aspects of a service can be graphically plotted against a base of time, for example number of outlets, specific features, number of sales, cost, or even number of producers, etc. (*see* Fig. 3.2). This will demonstrate which companies are leading or lagging

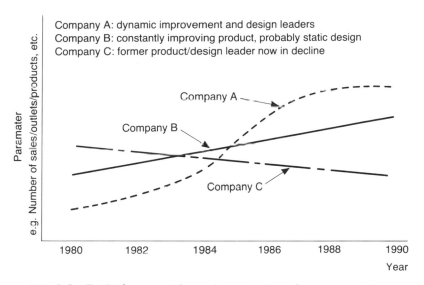

Fig. 3.2 Typical parametric analysis plotting changes over time.

in their design, in which areas are the greatest changes occurring or if the market is growing or dying. This may show in what areas companies are concentrating their design effort. Also, sudden radical changes in performance may indicate those aspects of the design that may have become dynamic and require further investigation. No change in performance over a period of time may indicate that a design format is hardening or even that the design is absolutely static. A declining number of companies in the market will also suggest that the design is, probably, static.

The second type of analysis is to plot on a graph any parameter against any other (*see* Fig. 3.3). This demonstrates where organizations believe the main market to exist, as there is usually a clustering of plots. Sometimes this is because of rationalization by companies. Often, it will be around the market leader's product, a possible indication that organizations are copying each other and are not doing original market research. It can also be an indication of a static product. Products appearing at the fringes of the parametric plot show where certain organizations are seeking market niches. Typically these are the smaller organizations which cannot compete in the main market area. They cannot confront the competition 'head on' and, therefore, find a less exploited section

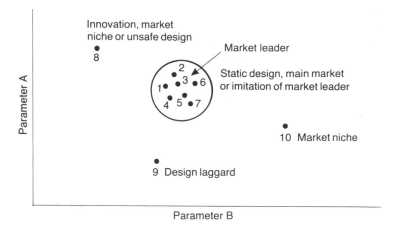

Fig. 3.3 Typical plot of parametric analysis parameter against parameter.

of the market. It may also indicate where an organization has innovated and these services should be investigated to identify what the innovation is and whether it is worth copying.

Of course, care must be taken to compare like with like. If it is difficult to compare products, because their parameters are so different, it may suggest that the design is dynamic, whereupon it is sometimes possible to identify the potentially dominant design, the one that will create the static plateau, if one concept appears on many counts to be superior to the others.

The best results are obtained by plotting as many parametric graphs as possible, without being selective about which parameters are plotted against which. As a broad statement, anything less than twenty plots is probably not enough to explore a product to sufficient depth, but once the data is available this need only take a couple of days.

The information from which the parametric analysis is made can be obtained from the product's own sales literature and from the industry's trade magazines. Parametric analysis, therefore, can show if an organization's design is better, more effective, more efficient or worse than the competition. Parametric analysis is also useful later in design for assessing a group of potential suppliers which are providing components to be incorporated into your service.

This form of analysis gives the designer a greater understanding of his service in the market compared to the competition, and shows where his organization leads or lags and where more design effort should be directed.

Another simple method of desk research is to take services that compete with your own, then identify which are the best features that would make a third service that is better than the other two. Again, this is best demonstrated by looking at a product rather than a service. Take two successful but different cars, the Rover Mini and the Citroen 2CV. The preferable features of each are:

2CV	Mini
Four doors	Transverse engine
Convertible top	Higher power
Low price	Small size
Bolt-on parts	Efficient use of inside space
Starting handle	Heated rear window
Battery charge indicator	Large windscreen
Air cooled engine – no need for antifreeze	Cheap spares
Effective suspension	

Can these features provide the basis for a third, low-cost, family car? Services can be similarly 'combined' into an effective new product.

With desk research you are acquiring existing data and, as such, most of this information should also be available to your competitors. Also, it may be out of date or not totally suited to your needs. Primary research costs more but will provide you with information that is probably exclusive to your organization and you can tailor it to your exact requirements. This type of research focuses on the habits, attitudes and requirements of consumers.

Interviewing

Interviewing is still the most widely used method of acquiring new information. This generally comes under two broad headings – qualitative and quantitative.

Qualitative research is carried out first and is exploratory and diagnostic. It is used to determine people's attitudes. As such it is hypothesis forming – that is, it provides the information from which a structured questionnaire can be compiled.

Quantitative research is then undertaken using this structured questionnaire to test the hypothesis. Quantitative research determines how widely these attitudes are held and the findings are usually expressed in numerical form.

The differences between qualitative and quantitative research are shown in Table 3.2.

Table 3.2 Differences between qualitative and quantitative research

Qualitative data collection	Quantitative data collection
Small scale (100s)	Large scale (1,000s)
Diagnostic/exploratory/inconclusive	Conclusive
Hypothesis creating	Hypothesis proving
Determines type of attitude held	Determines extent to which attitudes are held

Qualitative data collection	Quantitative data collection
Provides questions for quantitative research	Seeks answers to questions generated in qualitative research
Indirect interviewing	Direct interviewing
Personal	Personal, postal, telephone, computer
Relaxed, comfortable surroundings	Less comfortable surroundings
Informal atmosphere	Formal atmosphere
Recruitment by quota sampling	Random or quota sample
Semi-structured questionnaire	Structured questionnaire
Lengthy time period (1 – 2 hours)	Shorter time period (minutes)
Shorter time for total research	Longer time for total research
Tape recorded	Answer sheets
Skilled researcher	Unskilled researcher
Analysis difficult	Analysis easy
Cheap	Expensive

Interviewing takes four forms: telephone, postal, personal (face to face) and computer based. The personal interview is again subdivided into small and large groups. As it is qualitative the small group interview is carried out first and the results of this are used to formulate the questionnaire to be administered in the other forms of interviewing.

Small group personal interviews

These account for 7 per cent of interviews and are quite different from the other types because they, generally, do not have set questions. Typically, a group of about nine people will meet in comfortable surroundings and discuss a topic for about an hour. The group will be led by a trained psychologist, who will direct the discussion which will be recorded. Those being interviewed are, generally, paid a small fee (about £15). Analysis of the results is difficult and requires skill.

Computer-based interviews

This was first undertaken in 1978 and takes the form of a person sitting at a computer terminal answering questions that appear on the screen. These usually only require a yes (Y) or no (N) or a numerical answer and, therefore, the interviewee will not need keyboard skills. The programs are interactive, so that, depending on the answer given, a range of follow-up questions can be displayed. An example could be 'Do you smoke cigarettes?' If the answer is 'yes' the next question would be 'How many cigarettes do you smoke a day?' If the answer is 'no' a different question would be displayed next.

46

An obvious disadvantage with this system is that a computer terminal must be available and, therefore, this type of interviewing needs to be undertaken indoors, where a large number of people are available for questioning, for example at an exhibition. An advantage is that there is no interviewer to influence the opinions given.

Telephone interviews

Telephone interviews are the fastest growing category (currently 13 per cent). Originally findings from this method were biased towards the wealthier classes of interviewees, but from 1988 it has been determined that, in Britain, a random selection of telephone interviews will give a cross section of the population as a whole.

A famous example of the possibility of a biased sample was a poll undertaken by telephone in America to determine the likely winner in the 1948 US Presidential election. At that time only the richer people had telephones and the result showed that the Republican candidate (Dewey) would win. In fact the Democrat (Truman) won easily.

Telephone questionnaires are quick and easy to deliver, but the questionnaire has to be brief and exhibits cannot be discussed. Also, one cannot be sure who is actually answering the questions.

Postal interviews

These comprise approximately 6 per cent of interview questionnaires. The main problem with postal questionnaires is that they tend not to be answered. A return of 30 per cent can be considered good. This can be increased by making the questionnaire brief and interesting, as well as offering a reward for returning it completed, such as a small gift, a voucher for a discount, or entering the person's name in a competition. Another way of increasing the returns is by making the questionnaire come from a prestigious body or sending it to interested parties. For example, if the questionnaire is about dog food then it may be sent to members of a dog breeders' association. A follow-up reminder can also increase the rate of return. One cannot be sure that the returned questionnaire has been answered by the person to whom it was sent. Perhaps a secretary has answered a questionnaire sent to a manager.

One advantage of a postal questionnaire is that it can be multinational and multilingual. Once the questionnaire has been translated, as long as the questions are not open-ended there is no need for those involved to have a command of any foreign language. Postal questionnaires are inexpensive but take a relatively long time in getting the required data.

Large group personal interviews

This is still the most popular method and accounts for some 74 per cent of questionnaires. Interviewers using these will know that they are talking to the right person and the usual stimuli or exhibits can be used. This is an expensive form of data collection and the 'right' person may be difficult to locate. It must be remembered that interviewers may not want to carry out the work in 'tough neighbourhoods' and attitudes conveyed by body language may bias the results.

Table 3.3 gives a comparison between the four different types of questionnaire to measure attitudes.

Table 3.3 Types of attitude measuring questionnaires

Feature	Postal	Telephone	Large group personal	Computer
Sample type	Random or quota	Quota	Random	Random
Cost	Low	Medium	High	Medium
Speed	Slow	Fast	Medium	Medium
Length	Long (20 min)	Short (6 min)	Long (20 min)	Short (5 min)
Exhibits	No	No	Yes	No
Interviewer effect	No	Yes	Yes	No
Interviewer observation	No	No	Yes	No
Tough neighbourhood	Yes	Yes	No	No
Multilingual interviewer	No	Yes	Yes	No
Correct interviewee	No	No	Yes	No

Questionnaire design

The structure of written questionnaires

Decide how you will analyse the questionnaire before it is written. The questionnaire should always be as brief and as interesting as possible. It must be easy to answer and, just as importantly, it must be easy to analyse subsequently – the sample may include many thousands of people. In such cases open-ended questions should be avoided. The design of the questionnaire can aid analysis. Perhaps an optical reader can be used, so that appropriate marks on the answer sheet can be identified and counted electronically. Alternatively, the questionnaire could be in the form of a punch card, in which holes are pierced as the questions are answered. Again, the holes in the card can be 'recognized' and counted electronically.

Order the questions in a logical manner so that one topic leads easily to the next. If any embarrassing or annoying questions must be included position these at the end, so that if interviewees are offended and walk away you will still have their other answers. Use simple language: 50 per cent of the population do not understand words like 'incentive', 'proximity' and 'discrepancy'.

Prior to giving the interview there must be a short preamble that should be read out very carefully by the interviewer to the interviewee. This explains the purpose of the interview and is so designed to put the interviewee at ease. At the beginning of the questionnaire there should be a few questions that help to determine the socio-economic class or lifestyle of the individual. These include age range, sex (not for a personal interview) and the occupation of the main wage earner in the household (sometimes called, rather unsatisfactorily, 'the head of the household'). These are necessary, for example, if you are trying to discover what features a person wants in a luxury car – there is little purpose in asking someone who is unemployed. If the interviewee does not fit into the required market segment the interview can be curtailed. The initial questions should be easy to answer and become progressively more difficult.

Writing a good questionnaire is extremely difficult and it is vital to carry out a pilot test on a very small sample to see if it 'works'. Of course, the only questions that will be asked are those to which answers cannot be found by desk research. Some points to remember:

1.   Most questionnaires are completed by untrained people and thus must not require interpretation of answers or follow-up questions by the interviewer.
2.   Do not imply an answer in your questions (e.g. 'Isn't Blotto beer horrible?')
3.   Do not ask two questions in one (e.g. 'How do you think the taste and price of Blotto beer compares with lager?'). You may not be sure which answer relates to which question.
4.   Ensure that the question is precise and to the point.
5.   Do not ask vague questions such as 'why are you here?', which could be answered in many ways.
6.   The larger the sample, the more accurate the findings are likely to be? It is important to ensure that you are directing your questions towards the right market segment.

Designing a questionnaire that measures and gives correct scores on a customer's attitude towards a product or service must be done with great care. The following scales have been found useful for determining the attitudes of potential customers.

The Thurstone method of equal-appearing intervals

This method of attitude measurement was developed early in the history of attitude research by the social scientist L. L. Thurstone (1928). The aim of the researcher is to construct a scale marked off in equal units. Although the aim might seem relatively easy to achieve, the procedure for developing this kind of scale is, in fact, quite complex. Initially, the researcher develops a large number of statements about the object of interest, for example private health care, nuclear energy, satellite television, holidays. These statements are then rated by a large group of 'judges' who indicate their favourable or unfavourable attitude toward the topic. The rating is accomplished by asking each judge to place each statement in one of eleven 'piles', the first pile indicating an extremely unfavourable statement and the last pile indicating an extremely favourable statement. For example, if you were a judge in the procedure and the topic were attitudes toward private health care, you might place the statement 'Private health care should be available for those who want to pay for it', in one of the piles at the favourable end of the continuum. The statement 'Private hospitals should only be allowed to employ doctors and nurses they have trained themselves', might be placed in one of the piles at the unfavourable end:

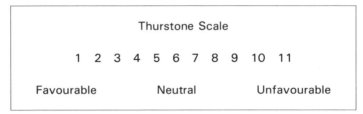

Once this initial group of statements has been judged, the researcher selects a smaller number of statements (about 20 is typical) for the final attitude scale.

Those statements that show considerable disagreement in rating among the judges will be discarded, the statements chosen will represent a spread of values (based on the median of the judges' ratings) along the entire dimension of favourable to unfavourable, with approximately equal intervals between pairs of adjacent scale values.

All this work is preliminary to using the scale to measure a person's attitude. Once the items have been selected, they are presented in random order (with no mention of scale order) to a sample of the population of interest.

Respondents are then asked to check those items they agree with and the researcher determines a respondent's attitude by calculating the mean (obtained by adding all the scores together and dividing by the number of scores) or median (the value that has as many scores above it as it has below it) of the scale values of the items checked. Thus, in the final analysis, an individual's attitude will be represented by some number between one and eleven.

The Likert method of summated rating

As you can appreciate the construction of a Thurstone scale always involves a lot of work and it is often difficult to obtain a suitable group of judges. Responding, in part, to the difficulty of using the Thurstone method, the social psychologist R. A. Likert (1932) proposed an alternative procedure for measuring attitudes that is considerably simpler and cheaper. As a result the Likert method has been more widely used in recent years than the Thurstone method.

When using the Likert method, there is no attempt to find statements that are distributed evenly along a continuum; rather only statements that are definitely favourable or unfavourable to the topic are used.

The researcher compiles a series of these statements and then asks respondents to indicate their degree of agreement or disagreement with each statement:

'The policy of giving membership of BUPA to an employee as a "perk" should be terminated immediately.'				
Strongly disapprove	Disapprove	Undecided	Approve	Strongly approve
(1)	(2)	(3)	(4)	(5)

A Likert scale will contain a series of such items and a respondent's final attitude will be the sum of the responses to all statements. For example, if there are twenty statements on the scale, a respondent's score can range from zero to one hundred.

In refining a Likert scale, a researcher will, generally, carry out a statement analysis to determine which items are the best measures of the attitude being investigated.

Specifically, the researcher will determine the correlation (the degree or closeness of the relationship) of each statement with the total score and will keep only those statements that show a substantial correlation with the total score.

The semantic differential technique

To varying degrees, both the Thurstone and Likert techniques require the researcher to undertake a considerable amount of development before a scale can be administered to assess an individual's attitude on the topic of interest. In contrast, the semantic differential method (Osgood, Succi and Tannenbaum,

1957) uses a scale that is general enough to be applied to any topic and asks the respondent to evaluate the attitude object directly. In this method, which was originally developed to measure the 'meaning of an object' (hence the term semantic), the respondent is asked to rate a given item or concept on a series of seven-point, bipolar rating scales:

> Place an X on the scale below to indicate how you rate the following:
>
> Private Health Care
>
> | | | |
> |---:|:---:|:---|
> | Fair | - - - - - - - | Unfair |
> | Good | - - - - - - - | Poor |
> | Valuable | - - - - - - - | Worthless |
> | Accessible | - - - - - - - | Non-accessible |
> | Moral | - - - - - - - | Immoral |

Any item – a product or service, a political issue, a work of art, a person, a place – can be rated using this format. The semantic differential scale has been found to overcome one of the problems of the Likert scale, that is the tendency of respondents to 'tick' the centre 'undecided' box. For some reason people rarely put their 'X' in the centre of a semantic differential scale.

With this variety of measurement techniques available, social scientists, market researchers and opinion pollsters have investigated a very wide range of attitudes. Attitudes on virtually every topic – environment, politics, religion, drugs, entertainment and many others – have been researched with almost every segment of the population. This shows the quantity, depth and variety of information and data that can be attained by researchers who use these techniques. These well tested techniques will, therefore, be of great use in enabling you to identify what potential customers require from your new products and services. Such information can be used with great effect in compiling and grading for importance the elements in the service design specification.

Observation

According to the Market Research Society Code of Practice, people may only be observed where they expect to be observed. Observation can provide a good amount of information at low cost and is most often used when people cannot answer, or are too embarrassed to answer, a question. As a general rule it should only be used for the collection of quantitative information as qualitative information is difficult to interpret. Observation in action can be seen in supermarkets where people's buying habits are noted. Quite often traffic densities or the number of single-occupancy cars are noted by an observer with a mechanical counter standing at the road side.

Observation can solve design problems. One example is the problem a refrigerator manufacturer was having with refrigerator doors. These were being broken by customers, although the doors had survived development tests. By observing how the refrigerators were used in practice it was seen that when the doors were open the users leant on them while reaching in to get the food. Redesigning to allow for this 'misuse' overcame the problem.

At a seminar John de Newtown (1990) described how observation was used by several companies. Honda observed people loading cars in supermarket car parks, which resulted in improvements to car boot design. When seeking improvements to electric razor design, Philips watched people shaving. A company that made newsreel film cassettes found that the cassettes were being broken. By observation they determined that the cause of the problem was due to users dropping bags, containing the film cassettes, from helicopters hovering over the news centre. The company, subsequently, redesigned their film cassettes to withstand this unanticipated treatment.

Another good example of the success that can be achieved by observation was undertaken by Russell Ackoff and his team from the Operational Research Group of the Case Institute of Technology in the United States. They investigated the siting of petrol stations in American cities, usually at crossroads where there are traffic lights. Ackoff and his team were asked where to position rival petrol stations. They observed that 95 per cent of car drivers entered petrol stations by three of sixteen possible routes:

Cars entering from the south and leaving in the direction of north.
Cars entering from the south and leaving in the direction of east.
Cars entering from the east and leaving in the direction of south.

This is shown in Fig. 3.4. It meant that cars could avoid the traffic light when entering or leaving the petrol station. The solution was clear: the new petrol stations should be positioned on the opposite corner of the most successful petrol stations in town. This was done and proved to be a very profitable decision.

In Britain too drivers rarely turn right across the flow of traffic to visit a petrol station. Generally they will keep driving until a petrol station appears on their side of the road. It is probable that siting a petrol station across the road to popular petrol stations on main roads would work here also.

When planning observation work consider whether the situation is to be natural or contrived. Will the respondents be aware that they are being observed and will this observation be done by man or machine?

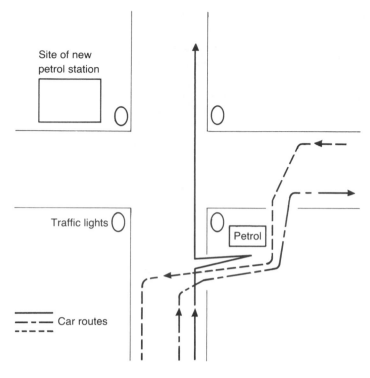

Fig. 3.4 Result of observing the use of petrol stations in America.

The advantages of observation:
1.   Co-operation of respondents not always essential.
2.   No bias due to questions or interviewer effect.
3.   Low cost.
4.   Effective for quantitative data collection.

The disadvantages of observation
1.   Cannot observe attitudes.
2.   Observer bias.
3.   Certain behaviour difficult to observe.
4.   Difficult to analyse qualitative data.

Providing there are set objectives, controlled and planned with results recorded systematically, observation can yield valid findings. Where possible have controls to ensure validity of results.

The ultimate purpose of market research is to evaluate the findings so that you can predict trends and propose directions for action. These must be presented in a report which includes a series of recommendations.

Report writing

The findings of market research and other stages of the design process need to be presented in a form that can be understood and assimilated by people in the organization. This is typically done in some form of report. In this section we describe the manner in which a report should be set out. The sequence proposed appears to work well (with small variations) for both reports in organizations and for the setting out of academic project work.

The general form of a report will vary depending on its purpose. For example, there can be reports of research findings, academic projects or a write-up of design work. The stages of a report, described here, originated from the generally approved format of a research thesis. This structure was then adapted to make a suitable structure for postgraduate management projects. The format was designed (yes, even reports must be designed) after various lecturers in the field were asked what information they needed from a report. This has been further adapted for business use. Not all the stages need to be followed, but we believe that the framework is applicable to a far wider range of reports than it would first appear.

A clear, well structured report can present one's argument and results in a lucid and logical manner. The tight structure makes the report easier to write as well as making it easier to read and understand.

Report structure

1. *Executive summary.* Four lines stating main objective and whether it was achieved.
2. *Contents.* With sections and page numbers. (Notification if relevant. An explanation of symbols and abbreviations).
3. *Summary.* Typically 1 – 2 pages giving an overview of the project, including conclusions and recommendations.
4. *Introduction.* 1 – 2 pages. Setting the scene. Background of the company and problems. Objectives stated in output terms, i.e. 'to produce recommendations on X'. Why the problem was chosen. Objectives to be broken down into their various components.
5. *Literature review.* Critical literature review structured to link clearly with the objectives and ending with an analytical framework of issues and models which will be used/examined in the fieldwork.
6. *Methodology.* 'What I did' in chronological order. The methodology should come out of the literature review.
7. *Results.* Presentation of data collected, if applicable in table form.
8. *Discussion and analysis of results* (may be combined with (7) in some cases). Referring findings and opinions to the literature review. Authors need only be mentioned in this section and the literature review.

Interpretation and assessment of validity related to the initial objectives perhaps presenting the analysis in Sections 1, 2, etc., related to the individual objectives.

9. *Conclusions and recommendations.* Tabulated if possible. Should be related to the objectives and answer the question 'where does this get us?' The conclusions must come from the evidence of the report.

10. *References and bibliography.* There are two standards that cover this. We have used one in our references shown at the back of this book. 'References' are referred to in the text, the 'bibliography' contains books and papers used but not actually mentioned.

11. *Appendices.* These should be short and relevant, not a dumping ground for anything that cannot be fitted in elsewhere.

Summary

- Marketing research is a vital stage in the design process. It should include:
- Secondary data collection/desk research – using existing information.
- Primary data collection/field research – acquiring new information.

- Various methods and techniques are available for the collection of information:
  - *Secondary:* Low cost, quick and easy. Examples:
  Listing advantages/disadvantages – for competition analysis.
  Parametric analysis – to identify your product's place in the market.
  Feature combination – to highlight the features of competitors' products that would make another new product.
  - *Primary:* Higher cost, slower and more difficult. Examples:
  Interviewing – Qualitative, to discover your potential customers' attitudes, and then quantitative, to find out how widely these views are held.
  Questionnaire – The design of these is difficult. They must be brief, interesting, clear and easy to analyse. Decide on which type of measurement scale you will use before the questionnaire is compiled. A pilot study should always be carried out before the main study is done.
  Observation – Useful for obtaining quantitative information at a low cost. Qualitative information is often difficult to interpret.

- The findings from marketing research must be compiled into a well structured report that is a plan for action. The report must be easily understood and assimilated by others in the organization.

Chapter 4

The service design specification

Introduction

Once you have established a market need, this information – having been determined through marketing research – is used with a great many other inputs to write the service design specification (SDS). This is the most important single document in the design process as it describes, in detail, all the relevant aspects to which the proposed design must conform. Just as the design model gives the design process direction, the SDS gives the design process breadth. It provides a mantle round the subsequent stages of design.

It is thirty years since Marion Harper (1961) wrote: 'To manage a business well is to manage its future; and to manage the future is to manage information.' This statement is more true today than ever. For information to be managed effectively it must first be collated, and this is the purpose of the SDS.

People in industry are woefully bad at writing down specifications, despite the fact that it has been known for many years that an inadequate specification results in inadequate products. In our research we have shown that it is possible to relate the market success of a product to the length of the specification from which it was designed. We visited various companies that manufactured particular types of product and asked to see the specifications which were used in the design of these products. Those companies that had the longest specifications were those that also had the largest market share for these particular products. The companies that tried to design a product with an inadequate specification were usually just trying to copy the market leader ('me too' products) and had not made a serious attempt to consider the design problem from first principles. This feature can also be seen from the plots of parametric analysis.

Compiling the SDS is an early stage of the design process and this is often undertaken before many 'traditional' designers become involved. Our finding shows that the route to market success is often determined very early and before the stage where some designers start. Furthermore, our research into the service sector suggests that the situation here is even worse, as some companies embark

57

on a new service without having written a specification at all. They have planned the service in a haphazard manner without a reference document, anything to aid planning or any criteria on which to base their decisions. They are not in control of their business.

Writing a good specification is not particularly expensive or time consuming in relation to the later parts of the design process. In spite of its apparent low cost, writing a good SDS is not easy.

The elements to be considered

With engineering products the elements that feed into the specification have been identified in broad terms and are shown in Fig. 4.1. This was developed by Stuart Pugh (1983) when he was at Loughborough University and slightly revised by Hollins (1988).

What we set out to determine was a similar group of elements that were applicable to the service sector. We therefore supplied a copy of Fig. 4.1 to thirty people employed in the provision of new products in the service sector and asked them initially to identify those elements that did not apply in their SDS's. Surprisingly, there were very few. Only patents and manufacturing facility were considered unimportant for service design. We then asked these people to add any elements they thought ought to be included in the list. These were: presentation (akin to finish), service facility, customer (may be different to user) training, skills/human resources, implementation, reputation/image of firm, entertainment/fun, availability, price (which is different from cost), communication (e.g. different languages), promotion, insurance, pollution, distribution, technical update, display and security. These elements are included in Fig. 4.2.

We then contacted fifteen people involved in product design in industry and gave them the list of elements shown in Fig. 4.2 and asked them to identify those which were not relevant to their market. Much to our surprise, the new list was found not only to apply to services design, but also to product design. Apparently the original list could be enlarged and the final list is more complete for both the product and service sector. Figure 4.2 is, therefore, the state of the art regarding the elements that must be considered for compiling specifications for both products and services. We know of no other attempts to identify what should be included in the SDS. However, Fig. 4.2 shows only the primary elements and should be regarded as a guideline from which you should develop a fuller list that better suits the individual needs of your company and its services.

When teaching this subject the challenge is offered that 'we believe all these elements must be considered in every design'. Usually someone can counter that certain elements are unimportant for certain designs – for example, patents are unimportant in a new financial service. This is true, of course, but the

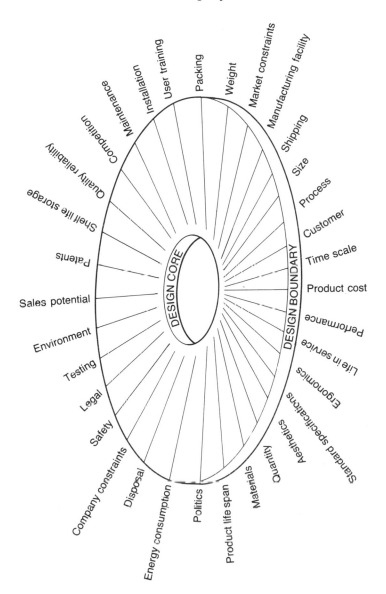

Fig. 4.1 Elements of product design specification.
(Source: Pugh (1983), revised Hollins (1988).)
Courtesy of *Patent World* January 1990.

statement was 'must be considered', and it is necessary to consider all the elements in turn so that it can be stated with confidence which ones are unimportant. The easiest way to do this is to get 51 sheets of paper – head one for each element – and then start to write about it. After a short time

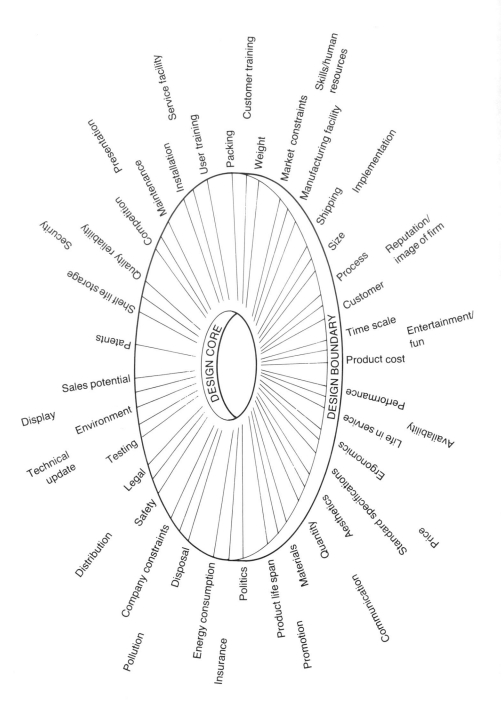

Fig. 4.2 Elements of service design specification.

it will become obvious which are unnecessary. More often those elements which initially appeared unimportant warrant a good degree of thought and managerial decision-making. For example, 'politics' is often ignored in specifications but changes in legislation can certainly affect the market potential of some products even if the legislation was not apparently directly applied in that field. For example, the EC milk subsidies of some years ago had a knock-on effect which meant that farmers had much less capital available for investment in other areas. Suppliers of farm machinery suffered as a consequence.

Another aspect, which will become apparent, is that several elements are dependent on others or are interrelated. The processes adopted, such as automation, depend on the potential number of customers, the technology available and the costs involved, as well as the facilities available and the actions of the competition.

Make your specification concise, putting down only usable information in a form that can be used by others. There is no contradiction between asking for a concise specification and stating that it will be long. If all the points are covered in sufficient depth, no matter how concise the writers have been, the document will be long.

Be quantitative rather than qualitative, where possible, putting a range on the numbers given. For example, the specification that 'Hotel corridors should be cool in summer' provides insufficient information to enable the heating and ventilation engineer to identify the air-conditioning requirements and is therefore bad. 'Hotel corridor temperature between May and September inclusive – 16°C to 18°C' is much better, as the heating and ventilation engineer has the necessary target on which to base the calculations.

A common error in the SDS is to specify parameters that are unnecessarily restrictive. This has a doubly damaging effect. Restricting certain aspects of design more closely than is necessary only increases the eventual cost of the product. For example, do not demand delivery to be faster than is really required. Parameters should be specified, but keep all such requirements as broad as possible so that they still meet the market requirements.

The other damaging effect is that an over-restrictive SDS can limit 'flair'. Putting a structure on the management of design doesn't mean putting it into a straight-jacket. The staff involved in the design of some defence equipment, who generally write excellent specifications, are at fault in this area. Those involved in design should be given enough freedom to provide some intuitive or innovative design, if at all possible. The SDS ensures that the overall design will still satisfy the findings of the market research. If, whilst doing this, the eventual design performs in a different manner to the competition, so much the better.

Several companies we have visited have had instructions on how to compile the SDS. Usually these documents are so restrictive that they could only be used to compile an SDS for a specific product. It may initially seem to be effective and faster restricting the SDS in this way, but you will only end up designing a service very similar to what has gone before. Something a bit different may, in fact, be more successful, especially if the resulting product is different from the competition.

The specification should never be written by only one person and all those who have a managerial role covering the various elements should provide an input. Total Design is a multidisciplinary activity and it is no longer the case that one person will have the necessary knowledge to enable him to provide all the inputs. Furthermore, research undertaken at IBM showed that when people wrote specifications they tended to put too great an emphasis on areas of their own expertise.

The iterative nature of the design process allows for specifications to be changed and updated as markets and circumstances change. This may even lead to the abandonment of a design if the competition brings out an identical or superior service with which your company cannot compete. Alternatively, you may be unsure about aspects of a particular element and in this case you may need to do some more market research.

Although changing the SDS is allowed, there is a point beyond which it is unwise to change the specification unless it is absolutely necessary. This is where good design management comes in: to know when to change the SDS and when to fix it to give some stability to the subsequent design process. There is no simple answer to this. You must aim to minimize disruption, but at the same time keep the design on target to be a successful product. Updating and changing a specification naturally causes disruption and the later in the design process that the changes are made, the greater will be the disruption and its associated cost.

In such circumstances an attempt must be made to identify the total cost that will result from the change in the specification and relate this to the anticipated fall in sales of the eventual service if the change is not made. Coupled with this the total cost of the change, or the potential fall in market demand if the change is not made, may make the whole design project unviable. An attempt must be made to quantify this also. Trying to quantify these scenarios in financial terms is very difficult to do in practice. Only a design manager with a very good control of existing and potential design costs will be able to do this accurately, but it is always important to make the attempt. Whenever you have a change you must put an issue number and date on it.

There is another failing of some specifications: where constant changes – or moving the goal posts – prevents completion of the design or results in an over-priced or unacceptable product. This has been called the 'Nimrod factor' and it is difficult to avoid with products that are being designed at the leading edge of technology. If you are not prepared to confront this problem, then be second in the race so that somebody else is ironing out the unforeseen difficulties for you.

Subspecifications

The British Standards Institute is currently working on a *Guide to the Preparation of Specifications* and this will give an excellent direction to the writing of specifications for the service sector as well as for industry.

One recommendation of the British Standard is that there should be several specifications for a product. This is also one of the main findings of our research. Several 'subspecifications' are required and these must be compiled by different subgroups of the design team to clarify and specify particular aspects of the early stages of the design. These subgroups will usually be responsible for implementing the relevant stage. These subspecifications will let all involved in the design process know what others are doing. They can then be used to aid decision-making and to identify 'gaps' in the design before proceeding to the next stage of the process. They will also focus the discussion in the design reviews.

Subspecifications will be assembled into one complete SDS, co-ordinated by the product champion. This is the only person who will need the entire document. The product champion will also be responsible for ensuring that there is no contradiction between these subspecifications. Where contradictions occur, the product champion will call together the parties who drew up the conflicting subspecifications to achieve a compromise before proceeding further with the design.

The most important elements

Not all elements in the SDS are of equal weight. The important elements depend partly on the particular service that you are designing, but there appears to be some that are more important with almost all products

It is, however, possible to grade the elements in your specification for importance and the easiest way to determine these important elements, having identified your market need, is to focus your market research to answer the question, 'Why will customers buy this service?'

Some research has been undertaken in this area for manufactured goods by Rothwell and Gardiner (1984) of the Science Policy Research Unit at Sussex University, as well as Parkinson and Hollins as part of their doctoral research at the University of Strathclyde in 1981 and 1989 respectively. For these quite different types of product the following appear to be important (*see* Fig. 4.3).

Reliability

This is 'the ability of an item to perform a required function under stated conditions for a stated period of time' (ISO 8402-1986). It seems to be the single

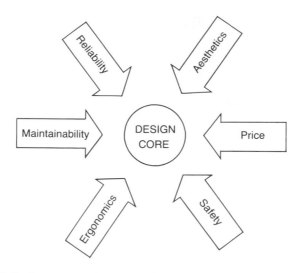

Fig. 4.3 Important elements of product design specification.

most important aspect of design in almost every product. For example, the most important consideration regarding a car is that it starts in the morning and keeps going throughout the day. When stuck on the motorway hard shoulder with a broken vehicle the fact that it looks attractive and has good aerodynamics is a poor consolation.

Reliability is often linked to quality (fitness for purpose) because it takes quality in 'manufacture' to achieve reliability. For a number of years, quality has been the most important design and production consideration among European manufacturers. This was discovered in a survey carried out by the French business school Institut Européen D'Administration Des Affaires (INSEAD). Perhaps surprisingly, a similar survey undertaken in Japan has revealed that since 1985 companies located in Japan have declared that flexibility, the ability to change aspects of their product quickly and easily, is more important to them. People in these Japanese companies have stated that this is because they have the quality problem sorted out and have now moved on to another pressing problem.

Customers quickly notice when a service is unreliable and it puts them off more quickly than anything else. They then tell their friends and soon the company has a reputation for unreliability and its sales plummet. It is to a certain degree possible to protect a company from a poor reputation by giving the service a separate identity, by giving it a different brand name, but this does not get to the root of the real problem. In your SDS don't compromise with reliability; make it at least as good as the competition. (You should know how good the competition is.)

What comes next in importance has not been so clearly determined by researchers but the following tend to come in the top six or seven main features of most designs.

Safety

This is the odd element out because, in most cases, customers do not consider safety. When they make a purchase they assume it is safe. Somebody who buys a plane ticket assumes that they will arrive in one piece. Although customers do not buy safety they do avoid anything they perceive to be unsafe, such as the Sinclair C5 or certain airlines that they believe have a less then satisfactory safety record. It is also the law that any product or service is safe, which only adds to its importance.

Aesthetics

This comes from the Greek for how something is 'perceived through the senses'. Nowadays this usually refers to whether or not a product has a pleasing appearance. Generally a manufactured product's appearance is important but the appearance of some services may also be important. For example, you would probably prefer to carry out a transaction at a place which has a pleasant, well-designed interior, where some thought has been given to its appearance.

Maintainability

This ease with which faults can be corrected is obviously important in manufactured products, but its importance is less apparent with services. The majority of services rely on and need manufactured products. If you are selling cars, dispensing cash or transporting people around the country, your service is dependent on mechanization.

A flight which has to be cancelled due to technical problems may mean that some of those customers will be lost to other airlines or other forms of transport. The perishability of the service requires that the plane is fixed as fast as possible so that other flights do not have to be cancelled. In some respects this very perishability of the service means that maintainability may be of greater importance and a short time to correct is vital.

Ensure that those products that interface with your service are reliable so they don't break down, but that if they do they can be quickly, easily and inexpensively corrected.

Ergonomics

This comes from two Greek words, 'ergo' meaning work and 'nomos' meaning natural law, and is to do with the people side of design. In America it is known as 'human factors engineering', in the computer industry as 'user-friendliness', but in each case it amounts to the same thing – ease of use. The interface between the user and your service must be designed so that your service is easy and obvious to use – and why not pleasant to use as well? We believe that improved ergonomics will be the main thrust in design during this decade and we describe below why we believe this to be so.

To make predictions in design it is sometimes best to look back on what has been successful. In Britain in the past ten years many new products and services have appeared crammed full of features we don't know how to use and don't really need. Examples of these can be found on videos, computers, telephones, word processors and TV remote controllers. If you don't need a function or it's not obvious how to use it, then it is bad design.

But look at the design successes of the 1980s – microwave ovens that are so simple and obvious to use, likewise cash dispensers in banks. Perhaps a good example is the camera. In the 1970s cameras were full of complications which only the professional could handle to achieve the optimum result. We slipped a decade and continued to use our Instamatic of the 1960s – drop in the film, aim and press the button. The result may have been misty pictures, but we could operate it. Now cameras are like the old Instamatic as far as the user is concerned, but full of 'invisible design' to focus and sense light, and incorporate auto flash and wind on. That was good design in the last decade.

So make sure that your service can be understood. For example, keep variations on booking conditions easy to follow – several travel brochures are extremely difficult, even for a travel agent, to follow.

If your instructions to operate your service cannot be expressed in a few words then you haven't designed the service properly. You are probably also losing sales because customers, quite rightly, cannot be bothered to sort out your inefficiencies and will go elsewhere.

As employees in many services have a greater personal contact with their customers than most industries, ergonomics certainly will be one of the top six or seven elements in design.

An old book, but still the best, on ergonomics is called *Ergonomics: Man in his Working Environment,* by Murrell (1969).

Price

Kenneth Corfield chaired a committee that reported in 1979 stressing the importance of 'non price factors' in design. This has led to the belief, in some circles, that the price of a product is almost unimportant in helping potential customers to decide whether or not to make a purchase. Although it is true that people often consider other attributes in making a purchase more important than the price they have to pay, the price of a service comes near the top of importance. People tend to identify a price bracket that they can afford. They then look at the various features that are available on products and services within this price range. They make their purchase decision on the item that combines the best of these features. For example, most customers will choose not the best holiday on offer but the one that combines the best combination of features regarding hotel and travel arrangements within a particular price range. So do not be deluded into underestimating the importance of price.

When writing your SDS you will find that you must compromise between the various elements in the specification. When you have identified the most important elements in your specification, through market research, you should not compromise on these. 'Derate' some other aspect of your design instead.

Needs and wants

With all marketing research, when potential customers are asked their views, they will have some features that they consider are essential (needs) and others which they would quite like but if they weren't in the service they would probably still use it (wants). In a way this can be compared to the work on motivation of Herzberg (1959). In his two factor theory of motivation he identified motivators (satisfiers) and hygiene factors (dis-satisfiers). In the case of a motivator, a person is pleased if it is present, but will not complain if it is not, whereas in the case of a hygiene factor the person expects it and will complain if it is not present. These elements must be clearly identified in the SDS as being either wants or needs. Try to include as many of these wants as possible but not at the expense of the 'needs'.

Some commentators suggest that it is worthwhile rating the 'needs' as being four times as important as the 'wants'. We do not advise this practice as this will lead to a belief that the specification with the highest total number generated by this means will lead to the best product. To show that this is not so consider the following. Do the fancy hubcaps, go faster stripes, good aerodynamics and central locking overcome the problem, in the eyes of the consumer, of an unreliable car which will not start in the morning?

Writing the SDS is an onerous business but for the subsequent model changes it is only necessary to 'top up' the information already assembled to take into account the recent changes in the market and technology.

The SDS is a document to be used throughout the subsequent stages of the design process. It describes what you are trying to achieve − it is *not* a description of the finished product.

One of the most useful books that shows where data can be obtained for use in compiling the SDS is by Wall (1986), *Finding and Using Product Information.* Its emphasis, though, is on manufactured products.

=============================== **Summary** ===============================

- The SDS provides a mantle around the subsequent stages of the design process. It is made up of at least 51 elements and all must be considered, although not all may be important with every service. The SDS will be an assembly of subspecifications compiled during the earlier stages of the design process. Compiling the SDS is a multidisciplinary activity.

- The elements can be graded for importance or listed into 'needs' and 'wants'. Generally the most important elements are: reliability (achieved through quality), safety, aesthetics, maintainability and ergonomics.

- The SDS will highlight interrelationships and compromises between elements. Do not compromise on the most important elements.

- The SDS must be concise and quantitative rather than qualitative where possible.

- Although changes to the SDS will occur in the subsequent stages of the design process these changes will become more costly the later that they are made. Try to avoid or evaluate the effect of any late changes to the SDS.

Chapter 5

Creativity – finding and assessing new concepts

Introduction

Throughout this book we emphasize the structure of the design process and the need for control at every stage. Designs must be constrained by the market and the design specification. We must design what people want, but this should not restrict thinking about the different ways in which this market need can be achieved. The design specification is a mantle and within that mantle creativity should be given a free reign.

Many definitions of design describe it as a creative process, using such words as 'flair' and 'intuition' to describe the role and personality of the designer. 'Creativity is the thinking process that helps us to generate ideas' (Majaro, 1990). The concept stage is where this creativity is encouraged unrestrainedly. This is to be welcomed if all the possible (and improbable) concepts are to be identified and explored.

Much has been written about the part that chance and good luck play in inventions. Certainly luck has a hand in providing good ideas but good ideas are more than serendipity. Alexander Fleming had a 'lucky' breakthrough when he noticed the mould on the sample dish that eventually led to the discovery of penicillin. But how many of us would have just washed up the dish and gone on to something else? Up to a point we make our own luck and only by knowing what he was looking for did Fleming capitalize on this piece of 'luck'. Have a clear idea in your mind of the area you are seeking so you too can capitalize on such 'luck'.

Thomas Edison was one of the greatest inventors of all time. He included the phonograph multiplexing telecommunications and improvements to the electric light bulb amongst his 1,300 patented inventions. Edison said that invention was 10 per cent inspiration and 90 per cent perspiration. It must be remembered that Edison had far more design failures than successes and practically all organizations in today's industrial world. Edison was unusual in as much as he carried out a lot of market research prior to developing his inventions. Too many designs and designers start at the concept stage of the design process. Someone has a bright idea, ploughs in the required 90 per cent perspiration to produce a product and appears on *Tomorrow's World* – and that is the last that is heard of the product and, often, its inventor.

Some people have said that we start to lose our creativity after the age of five when we start school. As we get older we learn more rules, gain experience and come more to rely on familiarity with the objects around us. All this may dull our ability to think beyond the status quo to new, and possibly better, ways. Even language can restrict our perception of things; for example, in French the same word is used for safety and security. Having worked on the design of safety equipment which prevented people having accidents in factories, devices such as valve interlocking and machine access guards could be overridden (with some difficulty) and so were not suitable as security devices to stop theft. The lack of differentiation in France and Germany between these two quite different concepts meant that when exporting to these countries it was quite difficult to put across the message that these devices would keep a machine or plant safe but would not prevent theft.

As we get even older and brain cells die, we are led to believe that we are less able to cope with change. Fortunately, John Harvey-Jones, a former Chairman of ICI, instigated research that has shown that older people are able to master new technology, such as the use of computers, as young people are, but it has a lot to do with the way the teaching is carried out – more time is needed and 'hands on' training is more effective – and whether the trainee believes he can do it.

Everybody can be creative. It is simply a case of teaching people how to be open to experiences beyond their own, however absurd these may seem. Allow them the opportunity to use their creative skills and give them the environment in which they can be creative. It does no harm at this stage of the design process to consider the ridiculous. This is because you have a design specification and, if the ridiculous ideas and concepts fall outside its scope, it will soon become obvious and they can be ditched. But if these concepts fulfil the requirements of the specification you may have a winner on your hands. These concepts can all be assessed, as will be shown later in this chapter.

Consider the example given by Tony Buzan (1984) on writing down all the uses for paper clips – starting with holding pieces of paper together. Ideas then progress to using it as a hook to hang up a coat, as a button, a bookmark, ear-ring, radio aerial, lock pick and so on. It then progresses to using several paper clips, such as a fishing line with a hook on the end, a dog lead, rattle, or Christmas decoration. Why not change the material properties and make a magnet or compass? Why not change the size to make ice skates, or the material to make biscuits? Or why not go to the extreme and first melt them down to make something else, like a saucepan? The Civil Service has found that only half the paper clips they purchase are used for holding papers together, the rest seem to be used for any number of things. Perhaps, some have already been mentioned.

Having got over this creative barrier it can be quite difficult to think of things for which a paper clip cannot be used. It cannot be used to make the sun shine, as microwaves. The things it can be used for may not be the best; on the other hand, just occasionally, they may be. Why stop at paper clips? What about all the things you can do with a brick, handkerchief, an extra finger (it doesn't have to be on your hand), etc.

We find this exercise fun and it serves the function of breaking down barriers built up over many years. People involved are less blinkered when they have to apply their creative 'talents' to more important tasks. Using the information in this chapter will help you to stimulate yourself and others to use your creative skills to their ultimate advantage.

Who are the creative people?

There are people who are creative and people who have not been trained to be creative, although everyone has the *potential* to be creative. The generation of ideas and concepts is dependent on a variety of other variables, particularly that of being in an environment which encourages an individual to get the 'blinkers off' and let the creative process flow in any way.

Problem-solving usually involves two phases: examining alternative solutions, then choosing the one that seems most appropriate. The first phase – recalling possible solutions or conjuring up new ones – has been called *divergent thinking*, the individual's thoughts 'diverge' along a number of different paths. The second phase – applying one's knowledge and the rules of logic in order to narrow the possibilities and 'converge' on the most appropriate solution – has been called *convergent thinking* (Guildford and Hoepfner 1971).

In solving difficult problems, people often alternate between the two modes of thought. When initial solutions are discarded as inappropriate, it is necessary to do additional divergent thinking – that is, to conceive of new possibilities. Divergent thinking is more closely associated with originality and creativity.

Some experts, e.g., Crockenburg (1972), have proposed a threshold model of creativity. The 'threshold model' of creativity suggests that a certain level of intelligence is necessary before an individual can make a creative contribution in his or her line of work (discovering a new scientific principle, inventing a new mechanical device, writing a poem or play). Beyond that threshold creative achievement depends on other factors – the fluency of ideas as well as other personality variables:

1. Allowing oneself to be open to experience.
2. Internal evaluation – developing the ability to toy with elements and concepts.
3. Being tolerant of ambiguity.
4. Having the determination to master the working environment.

5. Freely accepting ideas that people offer (it is non-creative to suppress them).
6. Being curious.
7. Having a willingness to work hard to solve problems.

It is, therefore, possible for anyone to develop the behaviour which will encourage their creative powers.

The humanist psychologist, Carl Rogers, criticizes western culture as reinforcing conformity instead of originality. The creative process depends on the existence of materials, events and circumstances as well as on the individual. This would suggest that the environment in which the designers work is also of importance to their creativity.

It has been proved that the two sides of the brain perform different functions. The right side mediates perceptual insight – images, colour, spacial recognition, rhythm, music, imagination, day-dreaming, creativity. The left side logically elaborates and verbally communicates that insight – reasoning, logic, language, numeracy, analysis, abstract thought. As we cannot directly observe the operation of the human brain, only consider the results, theories on how we think can at best be subjective. Knowing which side of the brain performs which function does not seem to be particularly useful to designers – how can they use the right side of their brains more? This would also suggest that estate agents would be heavily left dominated, but consider how 'creative' they can be when selling a house. Their description of a poor hovel that sounds like a veritable palace may be considered an 'artistic masterpiece' of creativity.

James L. Adams (1987), an engineer by training and now chairman of the Values, Technology, Science and Society Program at Stanford University, has written an excellent book on creative problem solving. He says:

> Bold and seemingly strange ideas, although they need to be subjected to ruthless and realistic criticism, often lead to the best solutions to difficult problems.
> Yet most people are inhibited by intellectual or emotional blocks, by the traditions of their culture or the group they work with or by 'using the wrong language'. They fall back on tried and tested methods – and come up with stereotyped solutions.

You can improve on your own present level of creative ability by developing the skills and behaviour needed, by working in an encouraging environment and by 'practising' and exercising the creative functions of your brain.

Barriers to creativity

There are barriers to creativity which you need to remove in order to be more creative than you already are. It is essential to remove these barriers if ideas and concepts are to flourish and develop into a successful outcome.

You should have already removed the major barrier, the one we impose on ourselves – the negative attitude of 'I am not a creative person'. Always think of yourself as a creative person. You have then already become more positive in your approach to new ideas and thoughts.

Convergent thinking

If you are a convergent or analytical thinker you tend to think that there is only one answer and all your ideas have to fit into an established pattern. Break away from the pattern and new ideas and concepts may emerge.

Choosing the obvious route/accepting the status quo

The obvious answer is the easiest and simplest to choose, but this is not always the best answer. If you challenge the existing and obvious methods a lot more better ideas will present themselves.

Fear of appearing stupid

There is a great deal of pressure put on us by others to conform – we are all afraid of looking foolish. But often what, at first, appears to be ridiculous can be a very successful concept. By putting forward all ideas be they silly or sensible opens up the 'floodgates', helping us to make connections and stimulate other ideas.

Rejecting ideas too soon

When ideas pop into our heads we have a tendency to dismiss them too quickly – 'that won't work', 'that's a ridiculous idea'. Many of these ideas may be refined and developed into something that will work or isn't ridiculous, that otherwise we will miss out on. Take time to consider the positive aspects of these ideas and thoughts before you reject them.

There are other barriers to creativity that occur in organizations that have been identified by Kanter (1983) and improved by John de Newtown (1990):

1. Regarding ideas from 'below' with suspicion.
2. Creating an impressive hierarchy of management.
3. Encouraging inter-departmental rivalry.
4. Treating problem identification as failure.
5. Expressing criticism freely and withholding praise.

6.   Centralizing the control of everything.
7.   Making important decisions in secret.
8.   Accepting no information without strong justification.
9.   Delegating unpleasant decisions downward.
10.   Never forgetting that top management know all the answers.

Clearly, all of these barriers must be swept away if the design process in your company is to flourish. The structure of design teams, as described later in this book, will do much to eliminate or avoid these barriers.

══ Finding new concepts and generating ideas ══

There are several ways in which individuals can stimulate their creativity. Here are some of them.

Challenge

Things don't have to be done the way they were in the past. Examine your service to see if there are other better ways of providing it or improving on it. Anita Roddick, founder of the Body Shop chain of shops, is said to have developed her idea from the 'I could do that, but better' concept.

Transfer

Look at the processes and products that you are familiar with or used to working with. Can they be applied to other services? Can the techniques used successfully in other areas be applied to your business. For example, can products offered by the tourist or leisure industry be used by the retail trade?

Checklist for new ideas

A checklist is another type of list which can be used to stimulate ideas. The checklist suggested by Alex Osborne in his book *Applied Imagination* (1953) is given here:

    – Put to other uses?
            New ways to use as is? Other uses if modified?
    – Adapt?
            What else is this like? What other idea does this suggest? Does past
            offer a parallel? What could I copy? Whom could I emulate?

- Modify?
    New twist? Change meaning, colour, motion, sound, odour, form, shape? Other changes?
- Magnify?
    What to add? More time? Greater frequency? Stronger? Higher? Longer? Thicker? Extra value? Plus ingredient? Duplicate? Multiply? Exaggerate?
- Minify?
    What to subtract? Smaller? Condensed? Miniature? Lower? Shorter? Lighter? Omit? Streamline? Split up? Understate?
- Substitute?
    Who else instead? What else instead? Other ingredients? Other material? Other process? Other power? Other place? Other approach? Other tone of voice?
- Rearrange?
    Interchange components? Other pattern? Other layout? Other sequence? Transpose cause and effect? Change pace? Change schedule?
- Reverse?
    Transpose positive and negative? How about opposites? Turn it upside down? Reverse roles? Change shoes? Turn tables? Turn other cheek?
- Combine?
    How about a blend, an alloy, an assortment, an ensemble? Combine units? Combine purposes? Combine appeals? Combine ideas?

Visualization

Day-dreaming and visualization are, probably, the first step in problem-solving or in generating ideas and concepts. Sit or lie somewhere comfortable where you can relax – use deep breathing or other relaxation methods if this helps – and get your mind working freely on your particular problem. Picture different ways of doing things. Ask yourself different questions and visualize the results of the answers. Use your senses, smell, sound, taste and touch – these can lead you to innovative and overlooked solutions. They are also useful in the solution of problems which utilize the senses (e.g. in the design of a service for the blind or a new fast-food snack). These senses also support the visual image and each other to clarify the total image.

We have found a hot bath and a glass of whisky an ideal environment for this method. You need not worry about getting it right first time or about the clarity of the solution – that can come later. Write your ideas down as soon as possible and discuss them with others, refining and developing them as you proceed.

Lateral thinking

Proposed by Edward De Bono (1982), lateral thinking can be used at the concept stage. Thinking in an oblique manner can do no harm, but concepts generated by this method usually fall outside the requirements of the Service Design Specification.

Group activities

The lone inventor is still a familiar animal, but a dying breed. As two or more heads are better than one, seeking new concepts must nowadays be a group activity. Although, as we have said above, periods of quiet reflection on one's own can complement this group activity, it should never replace it.

There are several group techniques that can be used to stimulate ideas. These are called 'design methods' and some are covered below. Most are aimed at seeking new manufactured products, but many of them will work every bit as well for services.

Brainstorming

Brainstorming is a group problem-solving activity. The rules were devised by Alex Osborn in the late 1930s – although in its basic form brainstorming is probably hundreds of years old. Alex Osborn was a well-known writer on creativity and the founder of an advertising organization in America. He defined brainstorming as where a group of people 'attempt to find a solution for a specific problem by amassing all the ideas spontaneously contributed by its members'.

The group should consist of less than nine people from a diversity of backgrounds, working on a particular problem and following strict rules and guidelines:

1. No criticism, judgment or evaluation of any kind. Always delay judgment of ideas to a later stage; this reduces inhibitions and eliminates the defeatist attitude that 'all my ideas are useless, it's not worth putting any forward'. Negative statements are not allowed; comments such as 'too silly', 'too stupid', 'not right' will lose you interesting, useful ideas as members of the group evaluate before giving their ideas publicly. There is nothing better than criticism to stifle and restrict creativity.
2. No dominating role of leader. Everyone has equal status in the group, ensuring that everyone's ideas have equal value.
3. The group is encouraged to think 'wildly'. It's easier to refine ideas later than to think them up in the first place. If everyone is throwing in wild

76

ideas individuals will be less likely to internally judge their ideas before putting them forward. Often, once thought about and modified, the wild idea may be the ideal solution.

4.   Quantity before quality. Lots of wide-ranging ideas is what is required. Their quality can be judged later.

5.   Members of the group are encouraged to use each other's ideas to build on or modify: 'Combinations or modifications of previously suggested ideas often lead to new ideas that are superior to those that sparked them' (Osborn 1953).

A brainstorming session should be co-ordinated by the product champion.

1.   Organize the session in comfortable surroundings at a time when those involved will not be interrupted by other activities that will divert their attention (e.g. in a room without a telephone).

2.   Appoint a recorder for the group, to write up all the ideas as they come in. Use wall space or flip charts so that all the members can clearly see the comments that are being made. (If using a flip chart do not 'flip' over so that pages cannot be seen.)

3.   Explain the problem to the group, but do not give them time to analyse it in depth.

4.   Get every member in the group to restate the problem as they see it. You will find that there are several different ways of seeing one problem. There are always other aspects or angles that you did not appreciate. You should then have a number of different restatements of the problem on display.

5.   Have a 'warm up' session – this helps to get the right atmosphere and the members of the group feeling comfortable. For example, ask them to think of uses for a pencil. It should start as being a writing implement and develop into being a piece of wood and a lump of graphite. Allow the group to get 'silly', encourage noise and laughter. The group members will then feel relaxed and comfortable with each other.

6.   Go through each restated problem getting ideas for each. The different ways of looking at the problem will 'cross fertilize' in the production of ideas and help the group members to look at aspects they would not otherwise have considered.

7.   Persevere when ideas seem to be drying up and when the first 'flush' of ideas is over. Give the group members time to think. This is the time when this method is most effective. When thinking becomes difficult is when the ideas produced are of most value.

8.   Do not evaluate the ideas immediately. Wait for a couple of days while the ideas or answers sort themselves out in your mind before evaluating and making your judgment.

Analogy

This is saying that something is like, or similar to, something else that occurs elsewhere, often in nature. Douglas Smith, at the International Conference of Engineering Design in 1989, described it as the '5 star method for thinking up ideas'. For example, electricity is like water flowing down a pipe and a resistor is like a constriction in that pipe. If you are trying to think up a new financial service what other service is it like. A bank could be considered like a reservoir with water (money) coming in from one source and siphoned off by another. A pretty basic example, but hasn't building societies acting like banks and vice versa resulted in a whole range of new financial services?

Delphi method

In this method a group of experts estimate the solution to a problem, then give this estimate, *with their reasons,* to all the other experts. In the light of these opinions the individuals in the group will modify their solution. After a few rounds of this method an acceptable solution can be reached.

This is easier to describe by means of a diagram. Consider the problem of estimating the optimum size of a new car park (a problem successfully resolved by the use of the Delphi method in the past). The technique is illustrated in Fig. 5.1. A, B, C, D and E are the experts and their estimates and reasons are considered by all the other experts at each stage.

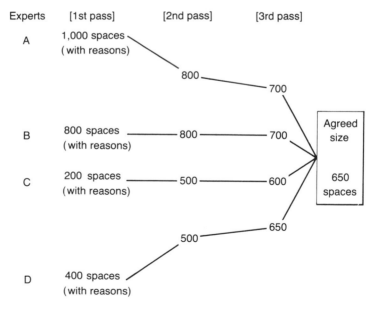

Fig. 5.1 The Delphi method – estimating optimum size of car park.

Morphological analysis

Koberg and Bagnall (1980) have devised rules for a 'foolproof invention-finding scheme'. In their book *The Universal Traveler* they describe their scheme which they call 'morphological forced connections'. These rules are:

1.   List the attributes of the situation.
2.   Below each attribute, place as many alternatives as you can think of.
3.   When completed, make many random runs through the alternatives, picking up a different one from each column and assembling the combinations into entirely new forms of your original subject. (After all, inventions are merely new ways of combining old bits and pieces.)

The following is an example of the technique:

Product: An improved bedside lamp.

Characteristics:

| Cylindrical | China | Separate shade | Bulb at the top, etc. |

Alternatives:

Faceted	Metal	Attached shade	Bulb separate
Square	Glass	**No shade**	Bulb at base
Round	**Wood**	Retracting shade	Bulb out of the side
Sculptured	Plastic	Built-in shade	**Bulb inside body**

Invention (but not a very good one!): A square lamp, made of wood, with no shade, with the bulb hidden inside the body.

The effectiveness of morphological analysis depends very much on the selection of alternative possible configurations. The example given above shows how ineffectual this design method can sometimes be.

An old book, but probably still the best, that looks at this whole area of methods of finding new concepts is called *Design Methods: Seeds of Human Futures,* by J. C. Jones (1970).

So, everyone can have new ideas, find new concepts and be creative. Assessing which is the 'right' or 'best' idea or concept that can be turned into a successful service is what good design is all about and can be the most difficult part.

Assessing new concepts

Trying to identify the 'best' concept is always a hit-and-miss affair and, like generating concepts, one can never be certain and can never prove that the final concept that is taken into production or implementation could not have been bettered. Several concept assessment systems are available and they each have various merits and weaknesses. Consider all of them and select the one with which you are most comfortable.

The concept selection system described in this chapter is a *concept assessment matrix* (*see* Fig. 5.2). It is relatively new and certainly isn't the simplest method, but it does have one main advantage over the others: it omits most concepts that will have resulted from the various design methods mentioned above. These are the concepts that are not right for your organization. The concepts remaining will be worthy of consideration. The matrix has been 'assembled' from the findings of various pieces of research so that the criteria against which the concept is judged are those most important at various stages of the design process and are also closely related to the market requirements of the product or service.

The concept selection procedure we describe was developed originally to meet our own requirements and we have found it to be very effective in our consultancy. Initially it will appear complicated but it follows a logical sequence which will produce a safe design concept that is suitable for your company and market.

1. In the first stage the safety requirements are considered.
2. The next stage certain concepts are eliminated that do not meet the company strategy.
3. In the third stage of the sequence the remaining concepts are graded against each other for various important (market) requirements.
4. In the fourth stage the best features are identified and combined into the overall 'best' concept.
5. A final stage ensures that the concept chosen still potentially conforms to the requirements of the specification.

This process is now described more fully.

Stage 1: Safety level

Section 4 of the Health and Safety at Work Act 1974 and existing and forthcoming legislation regarding product liability put the onus on companies and, more especially, individual designers to produce safe products. A haircutting machine that operates like a Flymo lawnmower may appear to be a great idea but the very hint that it would be dangerous makes such a product illegal. Therefore, any concept that appears to be potentially dangerous should be eliminated right at the start of the system of assessment.

Stage 2: Strategy level

Earlier in the design process the overall requirements of the organization will have been identified. These may include a requirement that any new product must be manufactured by the facilities available, must be sold by the existing sales force or selling method, or must be developed within a specified budget. All, or any, of these need to be considered here as well as other constraints that the senior management may wish to place on the company. These company requirements must be placed on the top line. These parameters should be definite – that is, if the proposed concept cannot meet or fulfil them then the concept is unacceptable to that company and doesn't warrant further consideration. For this level, therefore, all that is necessary is to indicate with a tick if the concept satisfies these requirements. The concepts remaining at the end of this stage then enter stage 3.

Stage 3: Market level

In this stage the remaining concepts are considered on a relatively superficial level with each other against particular criteria and placed in order of those best meeting the criteria. The best is given '1', the next best '2' and so on (some may be considered equal with others for certain criteria). The importance here is the criteria used. In Chapter 4 on the design specification it was shown that several researchers had determined that certain elements of the specification were more important than others and that it was possible to grade such elements in order of importance. Although design is full of compromises, one should try not to make compromises on these most important criteria. These, of course, may vary with the type of product being designed but generally the most important are likely to be: reliability (obtained through quality), price, aesthetics, ergonomics and maintainability. These are, therefore, the criteria against which concepts are judged. In your own market you may have identified additional important criteria and these should be added to this list.

At the end of this stage it should be possible to identify the overall 'best' concept that can be developed into a saleable and successful product or service. If there appears to be a tie between concepts then the one rating most highly in the criteria, reckoned to be most important to your company, should be judged the best. The chosen concept is then further refined in the fourth stage of the system.

Stage 4: Combination level

Although the overall 'best' concept will have been selected by this stage it is likely to be inferior in some aspects to some other concepts that received a '1' when judged against various criteria. In this fourth stage these criteria are listed and an attempt made, by combination, to build these into the chosen concept. The final aim is not only to identify the concept most likely to be a market success but also to include in it all the superior features of all the other concepts considered.

Stage 5: Specification level

Finally the chosen concept is judged to confirm that it still meets the requirements of the design specification. It need only be considered against the 'needs' rather than the 'wants' of the specification. This may require some adjustment to the concept but in practice it rarely does.

Throughout this section we have referred to the 'best' concept in inverted commas. The concept that you select will be the best one of those you have considered, to suit your particular company and market. It must also satisfy the important elements of your specification. But it would only be possible to be sure you have actually chosen the best by developing *all* the concepts equally, using the same investment in time and money on each, developing all the concepts into products and seeing which is the biggest success on the open market. No person or company is ever going to attempt that. Therefore, anybody who professes to have a method for identifying, or assessing, *the* best concept must be treated with some suspicion.

Another factor we propose that you avoid is the temptation to 'weight' one criterion against another. The urge is to state that, say, reliability is twice as important as price and three times as important as aesthetics (or whatever). The concepts are all then given numbers and the one with the highest numerical total declared the 'best'. In practice it is impossible to state, with any certainty, that various criteria are worth exactly that amount when compared with the other criteria. Those involved are deluding themselves if they believe that design is so simple that it can be rendered down to a mathematical formula or single number. A good manager will not attempt to do this but will bear in mind the aspects of the design which are most important. Ranking the criteria for importance, in your own mind, is allowed but weighting them is not.

Furthermore, it must be remembered that, like other management techniques, it must be used with care. The result you get out will only be as good as the concepts you feed into it. Remember, though, too, that you are the manager and if, when you have been through the process, the 'best' solution does not seem right then abandon it.

The service concept selection system that we have devised aims to compare concepts from three directions:

1. What the customer wants.
2. What the organization can do.

Creativity – finding and assessing new concepts

3.   Why it is better than the competition.

An overall plan for this concept assessment process is shown in Fig. 5.2.

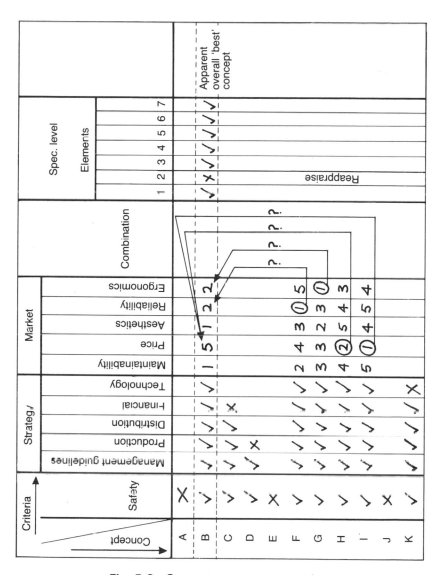

Fig. 5.2 Concept assessment matrix.

Summary

- Everyone has the potential to be creative. What is required is the right environment in which to stimulate that ability. The barriers which restrict the flourishing of creative ideas and concepts have to be removed.

- There are a number of methods that can be used to practise and exercise the creative skill.

- Various design methods are available by which ideas and concepts will be generated, for example checklists, visualization, morphological analysis and brainstorming sessions.

- There is no way to be certain that the 'right' concept has been chosen. The concept assessment matrix may be used to assist you in choosing the appropriate concept for your situation and organization.

Chapter 6

Implementation

Introduction

This chapter will describe the next major stage of the design process, the implementation or 'doing it' part of all the planning that has gone before. In spite of the varied manner in which new service designs can be implemented, in this chapter we can give some rules and point you in the general direction. Although the main expense is to come, the design should already be on course for being a success. Potentially unsuccessful designs will have been eliminated by this stage.

If this were an engineered product, in this phase you would be detailing the design, manufacturing it, then selling it. It is probably worthwhile thinking of your service in these terms. The concept is known, that is the framework of what the service is to be has been selected, and now it should be 'fleshed out' to include all of the elements of the service design specification. The 'manufacturing' stage is where those involved in this stage of the process start spending in a major way. For example, all the details of a new shop will have been decided and the property would now be leased, refitted and stocked for the start of trade.

The launch should simply be a matter of administering the plan decided upon as the culmination of the design process. There should be no problem with the service product, because all aspects of its design have been rigorously analysed during the design process. But as Alexander (1985) reminds us: 'Design does not sell itself but depends on the skills and commitment of marketing working in conjunction with designers to ensure the commercial success of the product.'

Following the launch the product should be monitored and measured against the original objectives. These objectives can, of course, be varied as new information on the market becomes available. Any variation from the plan needs to be investigated and the product either modified or some new product introduced to take advantage of any opportunities discovered.

Up to this point in the design process those involved will have accumulated

85

a very large amount of information and it will virtually all be in the form of pieces of paper. That's as it should be. As many as possible of the potential difficulties will have been confronted and overcome, otherwise the product would have been abandoned. A good design manager will have resisted the pressures to 'get out and do something'. Although having a model or prototype may give the impression that there is something 'concrete' to show for all the time spent, this should be avoided until this stage. In practice, once a prototype has been made, the emphasis tends towards modification of this prototype when often it should be thrown away and that stage started again. It is easier and less expensive to throw away bits of paper. Occasionally, though, a model clarifies understanding and can aid with the discussions surrounding market research.

At the implementation stage there is a fundamental change in the design process. From here onwards enough is known about the form of the final service and there should be sufficient confidence of the success of the final outcome to go ahead. Prototypes, detailed drawings and testing should all now be included under this broad umbrella of implementation. It is also the stage of the process when serious money is spent. From here on in the costs will escalate with a geometric rise in expenditure.

In our research we have found that, up to this stage, fairly firm guidelines can be given for most products and services. But after this the subsequent stages cannot be described simply in a few design models as services vary widely. Here design managers must design their own model that will describe what needs to be done to get the product on to the market and beyond. This must be carried out and agreed by all involved before this stage has been reached.

Having completed the Total Design process correctly, new models of existing products will take even less time. Having carried out the groundwork properly when the product was first designed, subsequent models will only involve a 'topping up' process to update the information. Ken Wallace (1989), who is responsible for lecturing on design and its management at Cambridge University, reminds us that 'design is seldom right first time' and that 'improvement is always possible'. Incorporating as many of these improvements into the design is one of the lessons to be learnt. Even so, as technology changes, often becoming more complex, and familiarity with all the interrelated aspects grows, so will the number of improvements.

Getting your service known

The 'selling' stage is the moment of truth when you understand whether or not your design has been a success. But, however good a service is, it won't sell itself. Promotion is an integral part of the selling stage. Potential customers must know that the product exists. Paul Cook (1990), the founder of Raychem Corporation, says that innovation is as much about sales or service as it is about products. These are aspects that ensure products are successful and are, therefore, all subsets of Total Design.

According to Cowell (1984) the purpose of promotion is fivefold, to

(*a*) build awareness and interest in the service product and service organization;

(*b*) differentiate the service offer and service organization from competitors;

(*c*) communicate and portray the benefits of the services available;

(*d*) build and maintain the overall image and reputation of the service organization;

(*e*) persuade customers to buy or use the service.

The form of the promotional mix must suit the service product being offered. It is a misguided belief that it is possible to persuade people to buy through some clever form of advertising. To do this is extremely expensive and, usually, results in failure. None but the richest organizations can indulge in or afford the heavy promotion requirements to make this strategy work. Even if you do persuade people to make a purchase, unless the service fulfils their expectations they are unlikely to re-purchase, and re-purchases are essential for the survival of a service.

As the service is new, the main emphasis of promotion must be to inform the potential customer of its existence. This is especially important if the service is an innovation, that is, the first of its type on the market. In such cases, it may be necessary to train potential customers how to use the new service. Often, it is quite sufficient to give written instructions. With more complicated services, such as scuba diving or car driving, formal training will need to be given and this training may even be the service on offer.

Most new services are likely to be an update on, or similar to, something that already exists. This being the case, most potential customers will already be familiar with them. Then it is only necessary to give general instruction on the new aspects and features of the new design.

After a period of time the form of promotion will change, from informing potential customers of the existence of the service, to reminding them of its attractive features. These will be the unique selling points that make your service superior to the competition.

Most companies fail to promote their services adequately. There are many stages in making your service known to potential customers before embarking on the really expensive forms of promotion, such as TV advertising.

Initially, identify the geographical area over which your service is likely to attract customers. This can be quite small. For example, if you are a window cleaner, there is little to be gained by promoting your service over a wider area than you are prepared to cover. In this case you can draw a circle on a map of the local area that is within easy reach of your home. In this area you can concentrate your promotional effort.

There are lots of low cost methods available to advertise your service depending on the size of your 'organization'. A starting point is the postcard in the newsagent's window, or loudspeaker announcements. The former often suits the one person operation, such as cleaning or odd jobs; the latter is not recommended, except for ice-cream sales and the like. The company van should display the name of the company, a contact address and telephone number. (Keeping the van clean will improve your image.) A staff uniform can also help to bring the company name to mind.

If you are to be out during the day you should invest in an answerphone so as not to miss potential customers trying to make appointments. The next stage up is a fax machine.

You should endeavour to match your promotional effort with your ability to cope with the work that results from it. Having more customers than you can cope with may sound like an ideal situation, but this can cause more problems than benefits. You start to overwork, rush the jobs to get more in and start to become unreliable.

Promotion takes many forms. Business cards and headed note paper are part of the mix, but these generally only 'impress' people you are already in contact with. Handbills through letterboxes are an effective next stage of promotion. They do tend to be read, if only briefly, so keep the message simple. Although the printing of these leaflets may be low cost, your time spent in posting them will be high. Newsagents will include these notices with the free weekly papers for a small fee.

To cover a wider area, advertise in the local newspaper or even the national press if your organization is large enough. The cost is proportional to the size of the advertisement and the newspaper. An advertisement in your particular trade journal can be effective – as long as you are not just informing your competitors who will also be reading the trade journal. Ensure your advert is placed next to an article and not just next to other advertisements. Readers tend to flick through these pages.

The best form of free advertising is a press release. These tend to be read, but must be interesting otherwise they will not be printed. If you can, make a suitable story out of some unusual feature of your operation or the backgrounds of those employed in it. For example, if you run a restaurant it may be that you employ a chef who used to work in a top French establishment. They may have only swept up, but as you are writing the story you can emphasize the positive side.

The next stage up in price is the local radio. A few seconds' advertisement can often bring in a suitable return of customers. Cinema advertising can also be focused on a local or national audience, although local cinema advertising tends to portray a somewhat parochial impression.

A well-focused poster campaign can give nationwide coverage from upwards of £300,000 and such campaigns have been shown to increase sales. Trade, or other, exhibitions can also be an effective way to introduce a new service. Exhibitions do bring in interested people and, therefore, potential customers (and also competitors). Be sure that the particular exhibitions will attract enough suitable people to justify occupying your promotional and sales effort (and all the costs involved) for all the time that it takes to present a worthwhile display.

As the radius of operation widens the costs increase. So always be sure you are not paying to preach to people outside your operating area.

There is a fuzzy line between promotion and selling. Your sales personnel should also be involved in promoting the service. They can do this by either calling on potential customers (cold calling) or by contacting them by telephone to arrange demonstrations. Enquiries should be met by a telephone call or by sending a catalogue, price list, or other information. A well-presented catalogue that gives all the necessary information in a clear manner is a difficult design task in itself.

Direct mail is sending unsolicited information through the post ('junk mail'). Its effectiveness is reducing as this activity grows. Such a campaign needs to be well focused and even then can be quite expensive if the cost of the usual inducements to purchase are included.

Yellow Pages or *Thompsons* will attract those who have decided that they already want the service but are not sure who can provide it. They will also show you who your local competitors are, people whose performance you must exceed if you are to be successful.

Interesting or clever 'point-of-purchase' displays will encourage retailers to show your service in a prominent place and customers to use it. For example, a cardboard camel that holds travel brochures will receive more attention than if the brochures were displayed in a rack alongside all the others. Other sales 'gimmicks' such as competitions, coupons, free samples, special offers, and two-for-the-price-of-one, all have their place in the promotional mix.

One should always attempt to try and identify if a particular form of promotion has brought in enough new business to make it worthwhile and justify the cost. This is not easy as one particular form of promotion is rarely done in isolation. Relating replies to various box numbers is one way that you can clarify which aspects of your promotional mix have been most successful. Guarantee cards or feedback questionnaires are useful in this respect. It is possible to ask a few questions on them which help to identify the type of people that are most likely to purchase the service (e.g. 'What newspapers do you read?'). Subsequent promotion can then be better focused on these customer types.

Corporate advertising is for promoting the organization rather than a particular product. This tends to be suitable only for large groups who want to establish a particular image in the eyes of the consumer, for example in giving an image of being 'caring' or more conscious to the dangers of pollution. This form of promotion is relatively new and there has been insufficient research to confirm that it brings in an increase in the organization's sales to justify the high costs involved. As it does not focus on one particular product it is not part of Total Design and will not be considered further in this book. In our opinion the best book on the subject is *Corporate Identity* by Wally Olins.

When deciding your promotion campaign consider the following:

1.   What is your customer base?
2.   What area are you trying to reach?
3.   What is your objective, specifically, of the promotion campaign?
4.   What can you afford?
5.   What is the industry norm?
6.   What are the tasks to be carried out and who will perform them?
7.   In what period of time should the tasks be accomplished?

And, perhaps, of greatest importance:

8.   How will success be measured?

Of course your promotion (including press releases) must be 'legal, decent, honest and truthful' as insisted on by the Advertising Authority. This means that endorsing the good attitudes towards your service must be done with care. Hence, the *'probably* the best lager in the world', 'nine out of ten pet owners *who expressed an opinion',* etc.

Pricing

The amount that you can charge for a new service depends, partly, on the competition and, partly, on how much it costs you to supply your product. Too often companies sell their products on a cash plus basis. That is, they work out what it costs to produce, promote and to distribute, add on a bit to cover overheads, then plus X per cent, which is the contribution to profits. This is bad marketing. You should charge what customers are prepared to pay. If your new design is an innovation you can and must charge a lot for it. For a start you have to recoup the cost of designing the service. Also you will have high introductory promotion costs to cover.

The method by which you 'manufacture' the service will, generally, be a new and maybe sophisticated process. You will also be at the beginning of the learning curve. Implementation is, therefore, likely to be inefficient with few economies of scale. The volume of the service provision, at the start, is likely to be small, and you may be unable to meet a large customer demand. As part of your market research you will have identified the basic shape of a supply and demand curve (*see* Fig. 6.1). As a result you will be aware of what customers are prepared to pay for the service.

The supply and demand curve does work. Therefore, by pricing high you

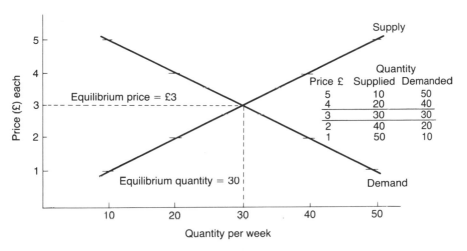

Fig. 6.1 Interaction of supply and demand.
The equilibrium price is at the intersection of the supply and demand curves,
i.e. £3. At this price the amount brought to the market by suppliers exactly
matches the amount demanded by the buyers. Above the equilibrium price supply
is greater than demand, therefore the price must be reduced to attract more
buyers. Below this price, demand is greater than supply which will result in an
increase in price.

can limit demand and, perhaps, even generate a luxury image for the service.
This will pay off the start-up costs more quickly. It is easier to lower prices
after a period than to hike them up. Such a pricing policy is known as
'skimming'.

The alternative is known as 'penetration' pricing, where the service is
deliberately priced low to keep out competition. This practice can only be carried
out successfully by larger organizations, who can support this policy with their
other products. A small business can rarely afford the luxury of this option.
Skimming is the more usual approach to adopt.

After a period of time the price of the service can be reduced as your ability
to cope with the increased demand grows. If the service is successful, sufficient
profits will accrue that can be invested in designing the next model of the service,
or something completely new, or just to help pay off the cost of other failed
designs.

The ability to charge a high price depends to a great extent on the
competition in your area of operation. If the 'going rate' for mending shoes
is within a certain price range (you will have found this out early in the design
process) this must be the starting point on which to base your prices. You can
then increase your prices, depending on what other features your service offers
– for example, higher quality, faster completion, etc. As a rule of thumb, don't
aim to be the cheapest on the market.

Competing on price alone makes an organization vulnerable. Customers are often suspicious of the cheapest on offer and prefer to aim for something a little more upmarket. For example, few people buy the cheapest wine available in the off-licence. Without any knowledge of whether it is good value for money or not, customers prefer to start their purchase decisions in a price range at least 50 – 70 pence above the minimum price. This observation is true of many products and services.

Furthermore, only one product can be the cheapest. If you attempt to compete on low prices it only needs one organization to come in at a lower price and your whole *raison d'être* then collapses or you become embroiled in a price cutting war, which can only end when profits are non-existent and one of the organizations goes to the wall. In this only the consumer is the winner. It is far wiser to compete on other features.

As you climb the learning curve (*see* Fig. 6.2) you will become better able to cope with increased demand. (The learning or experience curve relates to a large number of industries. It has an even greater effect with services because there is a higher 'person' influence and a lower machine influence.) Prices can be allowed to fall but you should still be charging the maximum the market will stand. At this stage of the product lifecycle your organization will then

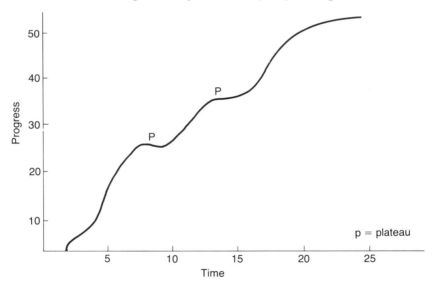

Fig. 6.2 The learning curve.
The graph depicts the behavioural changes that result from the learning experience. The rate at which learning is taking place, over a period of time, is presented in the form of the 'learning curve'. Achievement is plotted on the vertical axis, showing the measure of progress, e.g. time taken to complete a task, reduction in error rate, number of items completed, output per day, etc. The plateau is a period of non-learning, usually after significant improvement has been made and the learner moves on to a higher or more difficult learning stage. This is usually followed by a burst of rapid learning.

benefit from economies of scale. You will also have completed more process design, which is the design of the method of production or implementation. Also, prices will have to fall as competition will be increasing.

Eventually, at the mature stage of the product lifecycle (*see* Fig. 6.3) there will be fierce competition as similar organizations will be providing similar services using the same level of technology. Hopefully, at this stage, your organization will be involved in designing the service to replace the current one. You should certainly avoid leaving the next design until the decline phase.

Unusually, there are some advantages in still being in the market when others have left. If you still supply a product which is difficult to obtain you can carve out a profitable market niche. Until recently it was always assumed that prices fell when a product was in decline, but when there are few suppliers and a number of customers that must have a particular item not readily available, they will pay a lot for it. This is particularly true if the item fits in with some product they own, such as tapes for Video 2000, reel-to-reel recording tapes and spare parts for old cars. Quite a business can be made from supplying

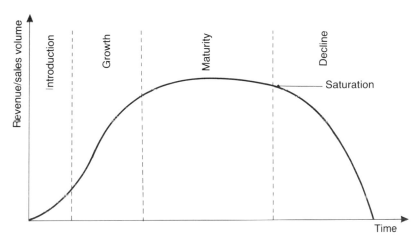

Fig. 6.3 The product lifecycle.

specialist markets. If this is the market you aim to be in that is fine. Avoid being left behind to fight for those declining markets through bad planning.

Evaluation

As the customers use the service it will become increasingly apparent if and where changes need to be made. Terry Maher, chairman of Pentos PLC, in a talk he gave at the London Business School (1990) summed up this evaluation well when he said:

1. Is the business a success, i.e. is it returning something?
2. Does it touch people's emotions, i.e. make them feel good?

Consideration of this is not a bad starting point. The service must be critically appraised to ensure that both the organization and the customers are entirely satisfied. This evaluation should take the form of a review carried out by the senior members of the design circle.

C. Merle Crawford (1987) has stated that: 'After launch the entire project must be reviewed to see how successful the team was, what problems they faced, and what they can learn to facilitate the next project.' This review will mainly focus on an investigation into the profitability of the service and market research into customers' opinions of it.

Redesign

Your service is now on the market. Customers have seen it and appraised it. So has the competition and, hopefully, they are trying to copy it – imitation, after all, is the finest form of flattery. This should not concern you, for, whilst they are copying your 'mark 1' service, you have started to design the 'new, improved, mark 2'. The competition will enter the market with a copy of your old service design about the same time as you introduce the latest form of the service.

However well you have undertaken the design process there will always be areas in which the design is deficient and this will only become apparent when the product is placed on the market. Therefore, as soon as a service is ready for the market, research must begin again. This will take the form of finding out what potential customers like or dislike about the product. Many of the techniques from the original market research stage can be used but some additional ones can also be included here. This is because customers have been using your service and they can provide you with feedback or relate directly to it.

A crude way of doing this is through customer complaints, but by the time a customer complains it is usually too late. Often people are bad at complaining. Rather than face the embarrassment of a confrontation they prefer to 'vote with their feet' and will either cease further purchases or go elsewhere. Endeavour, by pre-launch trials, to find out as many customer objections as possible before the service enters the market.

Of course, most of the design process will be repeated, in part, several times during the life of the service as it is periodically updated. Usually, in such cases, not everything needs to be redesigned and most of the SDS will survive with only small changes to match up with changing markets and customer requirements. This is all part of the iteration associated with Total Service Design.

The service should continue to be redesigned and updated periodically, until it comes to the end of its selling life. Long before a product enters the decline phase of the product lifecycle it is time to consider starting with a completely new product and the whole process will start again in earnest. The Total Design Process needs a feedback loop to remind you to start again.

Although we advocate design as being vital to any organization, avoid the potential problems that can arise through too much design. Customers like the familiarity of products and services and few, apparently, crave for constant change. If a product is continually changing this will confuse customers and prevent the development of customer loyalty. It also makes life more difficult for you! If aspects of your service appear to be popular, accepted and well used by sufficient numbers of customers, don't risk alienating them by changing these aspects. Concentrate on the less popular aspects. Some Japanese car companies have failed in this aspect of car design. They have reached the stage in the efficiency of their design process that they can change the aesthetics of their models every couple of years. Customers are already being put off purchasing such products because they have something that is quickly out of date. Furthermore, controlling the supply of spare parts in such situations can become a nightmare. Services are less likely to be affected by such problems, but don't ignore the 'comfort' that familiarity can provide. In short, don't over-design.

Experimentation

Experimentation, in the marketing sense, tends to determine potential customers' attitudes, such as their perceived view of the status or quality of a (proposed) product. The most commonly used experiments are organized around existing products. One point worth noting is that attitudes held by potential customers may not be accurate, but in the marketing sense they are the truth. Having determined the customers' attitudes to your product, attempts can be made either to endorse or to change these views. This can often be achieved through some form of promotion such as advertising.

Kelly's Repertory Grid is a good method to use to ascertain individuals' attitudes toward your product. People are asked to compare one product with two others. Your product or, less effectively, a competitor's product, can be the odd one out. For example, 'State the differences between Margate and Blackpool compared to Worthing as a holiday destination.' Initially the respondents will state the more obvious physical differences such as:

'Worthing is further south than the other two.'
'Worthing is smaller than the other two.'
'Worthing hasn't any illuminations.'

Then people will begin to discuss their attitudes and this is the more useful information, for example:

'Worthing is where old people go to live when they retire.'
'Worthing is restful.'
'Worthing has no night life.'

If, in this example, enough people think that Worthing is a restful place, only suitable for old people to retire to, this image can either be endorsed or attempts made to change it through your promotion.

Another form of marketing research associated with the existing product is the Mason Haire Test (1950). Mason Haire was an industrial psychologist at the University of California. He suspected that the responses to a survey which revealed that housewives did not like instant coffee because of the taste hid the true reason for non-purchase. He prepared two shopping lists that were identical except that one had instant coffee on it and the other had fresh ground coffee. From this he determined that people perceived the type of person who used instant coffee as lazy, fails to plan buying, is not thrifty and is generally not a 'good wife'. The instant coffee manufacturer overcame this perceived attitude by advertising their product as one which allowed the housewife more time to be with and care for her family.

This type of projective test is still useful today. Give two different groups of prospective customers similar lists. Include your product on one list and a competitor's product on the other list and ask the customers: 'What type of person has written this shopping list?' This will show if your service is perceived to be more upmarket or downmarket than the competitor – that is, it will reveal its image in the market.

Total quality

Reliability, being the most important aspect of design, is reflected in the quality of the service. Murdick *et al.* (1990) state that: 'The quality of a service or product is determined by the user's perception. It is the degree to which the bundle of service attitudes, as a whole, satisfies the user.'

Total quality management is more than just a buzz word nowadays. Total quality focuses on providing customer satisfaction of a product or service. It is essential for the survival of an organization in markets where there is nearly always choice.

Total quality is defined as a management-driven but company-wide ethos to ensure that things are 'right first time' and have 'zero defects' and 'total conformance to specification'. These familiar phrases encapsulate a process of continuous improvement that becomes of primary importance at the implementation stage of service design.

But in addition it has been said that the quality of a service is dependent on the person providing it. To implement total quality consider the 'chain' of events through which a potential customer passes. Whilst using the service you provide, customers, to a greater or lesser extent, will 'impinge' on your organization and dissatisfaction at any point may lose you the sale or resale to these customers.

Consider students who wish to study at a college in the evening. This is the sequence through which most of them will proceed:

1. A student will telephone the college – often to be kept waiting. Don't let this happen in your organization.

2. Eventually the telephone is answered and the student asks for the relevant department, again, to be kept waiting. If the relevant person is not available the call should be redirected – quickly.

3. The next stage is usually a request for a prospectus that gives details of the course. Has this been well designed? Is it despatched promptly?

4. Having decided on a course, the student will make an application and an interview will be arranged. Are suitable directions given and meeting instructions made clear? The candidate should be met and taken to the interview room.

5. Has the interviewer been trained? Does the interviewer know what to look for in a prospective student and are the candidate's questions regarding the course answered?

6. The candidate should be promptly informed if their application has been successful or not.

7. If the college accepts the application this should be followed by further instructions, so that the student knows where and when to join the course.

There is nearly always fierce competition between colleges to increase class numbers so that courses can be viable. Yet it seems to be the norm that, having designed worthwhile courses, the colleges fail to deliver a satisfactory service to its customers before they enrol.

You may not be involved in education, but there are likely to be parallels between this and your service. Identify the customer chain and optimize each stage of this customer contact as part of your service. For example, if your telephone rings ten times before it is answered, investigate why and either retrain the staff involved or employ more so that this doesn't happen. First impressions are important – don't allow them to be the last. This sequence may have several parallel branches, depending on the service being offered.

Another example is shown in Fig. 6.4.

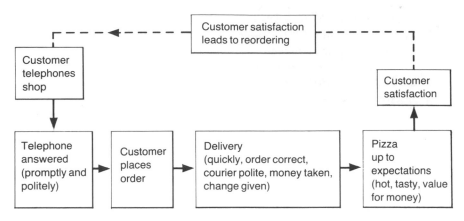

Fig. 6.4 The customer chain − home-delivered pizza service.

══ Implementation in the non-profit-making sector ══

One aspect of service design which is a little different concerns charities. In the non-profit-making sector, such as a charity, service design is still very relevant and, as we shall show, is in some ways more difficult than in the profit-making sector. We have found that those operating in this sector often have an unclear set of objectives other than 'to provide a quality service'. This may be the case, but what exactly is a quality service? By the strict definition this is 'fitness for purpose', but managers from this sector then go on to describe something more than this including the satisfaction of various criteria.

If the aim is to provide a quality service then what this constitutes must be identified. This can either be parameters that you set yourself as described by your organization, those set by your potential users, or those financing your service – or perhaps all three. This will mean that you will need to do some finding out, in other words market research.

One of the crucial differences of this sector is already apparent. Quite often those involved in the non-profit-making sector may have to do some market research on what the people who provide the money are prepared to provide the money for. This is different from convincing the bank manager that the money borrowed for the design of a new product is worthwhile as the bank is only interested in getting its investment back in a set period of time with interest. With a charity, investors can have very definite ideas as to where they are prepared to spend their money. Of course, your organization may be partly responsible for raising its own funds through various schemes and events organized in-house. Although, it will still be difficult to determine the return from such schemes, their timing and how the money raised is spent, will be your company's decision.

An organization in this sector must, therefore, do market research on from where their income will be derived as well as how it will be spent. This will be followed by two service design specifications to cover the way of generating income as well as the planned expenditure. In fact it may be necessary to have two complete design processes which will run in parallel. One will cover the income-generating side of the organization and the other will focus on the proposed expenditure. In certain stages, such as in the service design specification, they will be linked to each other.

The most obvious of these links is that the planned expenditure must tie in with the anticipated income. In charity fund-raising the amount of income can be difficult to predict. Furthermore, with some charities, the time of the year when these funds arrive can also be uncertain. This makes planning doubly difficult.

Planned giving and deed covenants may provide a steady income but government and local authority grants are often only assured for a maximum of three years and more normally for just one. Part of the desk research must be directed towards a determination of when, where and how much income has been donated in the past few (five) years. It will be found that this follows a pattern and money will derive from a few specific bodies and at particular times of the year. If the income does appear to emanate from particular groups then these, or others similar to these, must be targeted in your specification.

Looking now at what time of the year donations are made it will be seen that many charities follow a similar pattern as shown in Fig. 6.5. Income for much of the year is steady but there are peaks in April and September when companies make out their yearly and half yearly accounts and include a donation

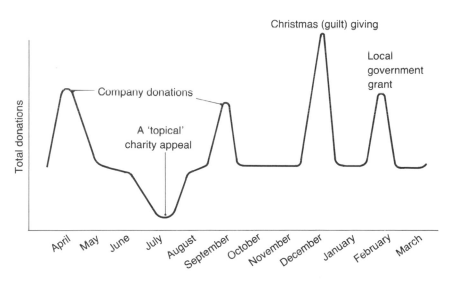

Fig. 6.5 Typical yearly variation in charity donations.

to charity (or a political party). There may also be peaks at other times when local government distributes grants.

The 'big' time for charities is around Christmas when many people give and this boosts the income of most charities quite considerably. The figure also shows a dip and this occurs when another charity dominates through being 'fashionable' for a period of time. During 'Live Aid', and also when the Great Ormond Street Children's Hospital 'Wishing Well' appeal was at its full height, the donations to other charities fell away drastically. This means that many organizations in the non-profit-making sector are in direct and fierce competition with each other.

Competition analysis must also be part of your market research. This competition analysis must be directed to find out who your likely competitors are, which may not be all that obvious, and also what they are doing in both fund-raising and spending. Apart from providing you with useful ideas it will, returning to our original premise, help to identify what is meant by 'a quality service'. Perhaps a level exists which is an acceptable service and the 'quality' aspect is that which is provided over and above this level. Almost certainly these two levels of service will be provided by your competitors unless you are in a service niche or monopoly. Compare the competition with your own service to identify areas in which you lead or can improve. This, initially, need be no more than comparing advantages and disadvantages.

Of course, both income and expenditure will comprise several discrete services that must be designed separately. Organizing a charity bike ride is quite different to organizing charity Christmas cards, although the basic design process through which each must pass will be the same.

There are likely to be several products that need to be designed for both income and expenditure even though the overall aim will be the same to fund, say, research into renal failure.

For facts and figures on 'company giving' and information for those seeking to obtain charitable resources from industry, *see A Guide to Company Giving,* edited by Michael Norton (1988).

Summary

- The implementation stage of the design process is the 'doing it' phase. In this stage the concept is developed to include all the elements on the SDS.

- In some cases a new service can be treated as a manufactured product, as it can be considered to pass through similar procedures:
  - detailing the design
  - prototype testing
  - manufacture or production of the service
  - selling the service.

Implementation

- The implementation is where large expenditure starts and therefore potential design failures should have been eliminated by this stage.

- During and after the launch the new product has to be monitored and measured to ensure that your objectives are being met. As new information from the market is acquired your objectives may be altered to take advantage of new opportunities.

- Getting your product known to potential customers is vital. Plan your promotional mix to suit the area to be covered and subsequently determine the success of the campaign.

- The price you charge depends on what the customer is prepared to pay. Initially your costs may be high and your price will reflect this. Over a period of time, as demand increases, costs and hence prices will fall. Consumers will pay more for an innovation as there is no competing service.

- Find out from your customers whether or not they are satisfied with your service. Small changes or redesign may be required.

- Total quality management is essential to ensure that 'things are right first time' and that the customer received a good impression at each contact stage of your service.

- Total service design management is just as relevant to the non-profit-making sector. In this sector it may be necessary to design the fund-raising process as well as the process of fund-spending.

Chapter 7

Innovation or incremental design in services

Is innovation necessary?

Innovation is defined as an invention in its first marketable form. If there is no invention then it is not an innovation. It is one of those much misused words probably due to it being wrongly used in advertising where every change in design is heralded as an innovation.

Although innovation tends to be regarded as mainly to do with technology, innovation is also an important aspect in the design of services. Drucker (1985) describes how American farmers, early in the nineteenth century, could not afford to purchase new machines for harvesting. Cyrus McCormick introduced the service innovation of payment by instalments or hire-purchase. This practice has become a major business.

We are often being told that if organizations do not spend more time trying to innovate they are destined to decline and eventually fail. It would appear that companies should be innovating all the time and that this book should be more about how to innovate than about Total Design. The media and government are pressing us that innovation is vital to a company's existence and headlines warn us that we stand to fail unless we innovate more. On the other hand we are also told that the UK is good at innovation but poor at exploitation of markets. Great products are supposed to have been invented here but the markets have been taken from us by other countries. In most cases this is a fallacy. Most of the time we have been inventing things that nobody wants, or at least not enough people to sustain a viable industry for these products. This is part of the reason for the decline of our manufacturing sector.

There is also a lot of innovation in the manner in which products are manufactured. This is called *process innovation* or *dynamic process design*. The Japanese are the masters of dynamic process design and we are a long way behind. Innovation is not a panacea for success – quite the opposite. It is something that should be well focused and used with care.

Innovation should be avoided unless it is absolutely necessary for four reasons:

1. It takes longer to achieve than improving an existing design.
2. It costs more to achieve than improving an existing design.
3. It is more difficult as those involved cannot rely on experience.
4. It has more risk attached to it, as it has a higher risk of failure.

This is because market research is more difficult to conduct on something new with which potential customers are unfamiliar. Market research should still be carried out, though, as few innovations are so absolutely new that potential customers cannot be questioned about their need for such a breakthrough.

These points can be demonstrated on an adaptation we have made of the curve by Buggie (1981) shown on Fig. 7.1.

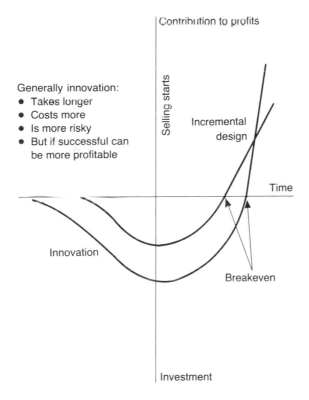

Fig. 7.1 The effect of innovation.

Innovation is not required with the majority of designs; with most products, at any one time, the concept remains unaltered. On the other hand, innovation with some products is vital in some areas, as we shall show in this chapter. If your organization operates in a fast-changing field where markets and technology are constantly shifting you must be aware of the changes that are taking place and be capable of reacting to them. Management must also be prepared to tolerate more mistakes due to people trying to work with the unfamiliar.

John Jewkes *et al.* (1969) (this book is currently being updated) have investigated the fifty-eight major inventions of this century. This ranged from penicillin to ball-point pens. They identified that the vast majority have emanated from companies that were not, at that time, involved in the particular product area. We believe that this is because most companies spend too much of their time looking only at what their direct competitors are doing. They all imitate each other then get taken by surprise when somebody new enters their market with something different. To avoid being taken by surprise in such situations, or, better still, to benefit from new inventions, your organization must take a broad look. You will only discover what is happening outside of your market if you have a mechanism in place to seek out possible changes. One person spending one day each month is usually sufficient to undertake this task.

This will avoid your company being caught out by new ideas and changes. Also, as you know your market requirements (or should) you will be in a better position to benefit from these changes than any 'interloper' as you have the market infrastructure already in place.

History shows that there is always time to make the necessary changes in the time lag between an invention and its acceptance on the market. As Foster (1986) has said, 'It is relatively easy to spot new technology on the horizon and to decide to monitor them or perhaps invest in them.' In this time lag the organization can either:

1. Buy into the new innovation.
2. Maximize profits with the existing technology and accept eventual decline of this product area.
3. Employ new people or train your own people who can cope with the new innovation.
4. Try and leapfrog into the next stage of the innovative process.

All this depends on the organization knowing of the forthcoming change.

Fortunately, with many cases, innovation in the service sector need not involve the high investment that generally accompanies innovation in the manufacturing sector.

The moral here is don't innovate unless you have to. Humble and Jones (1989) quote Peter Drucker as saying, 'The test of an innovation, after all, lies not in its novelty, its scientific content or its cleverness. It lies in its success in the market.'

But, if you have to innovate and you don't, your organization will be left behind. How do you know when you have to? This is a complicated area that perhaps can be clarified through the theory of product status.

Product and service status

Since 1985 we have undertaken research into the 'status' of product design. Product status identifies if innovation is necessary in product design. The original work on the subject was undertaken by Professor Stuart Pugh. In 1983 he proposed that Computer Aided Design was only effective for use on products where the basic concept did not alter. Where the concepts did alter, which is where innovation is occurring, it was more efficient to use more traditional methods of drawing. He went on to show that the concept of certain products, such as the differential gear, had not altered for many years, whereas with other products radical changes were occurring.

Hollins (1989) developed this work to show that it was possible to categorize areas of the management of product design into static or dynamic disciplines. This means that, if it is possible to identify if a product is, or is not, changing in an innovative manner, whole areas of the management of design become more or less important.

The purpose of product status is twofold. Initially, it enables an organization to identify if a product is changing innovatively or incrementally. Products that change innovatively are said to have a dynamic status and require dynamic design. Products that change incrementally or in an evolutionary manner are said to have a static status and require static design.

Secondly, having identified the status of a product, various parts of the design process become more or less important. These areas and activities, that can be expanded or reduced are known as *design disciplines*. Therefore, having identified the status of a product, those involved in design can concentrate on the important design disciplines and reduce their effort in other areas.

The most obvious of these is with the concept stage of the design process. If a product can be identified as being static then innovation is not required. This means that the existing concept is correct for the current market and, in simple terms, the concept stage of the design process can be viewed as unimportant. The concept that already exists is good enough and one can rely on experience and on what has gone before.

```
MARKET
  |
SDS
  |
CONCEPT          PRODUCT INNOVATION (if required) OCCURS HERE
  |
IMPLEMENTATION   PROCESS INNOVATION (if required) OCCURS HERE
```

The use of product status effectively renders certain activities in design redundant. It is one of the few techniques that actually reduces a designer's work. This, possibly, explains our insistence that organizations should not talk about innovation when they really mean design. Design is the total activity necessary to bring about new products, whereas innovation is only one aspect of design. It is that part which looks at the generation of new concepts.

Furthermore, when we say design is about products, it is important to focus on a particular product or product area. Otherwise an organization will be unable to identify and hence benefit from knowing the product status.

Many writings on design have merely focused on 'design' *per se*. Without a focus on a particular type of product, all that such writers can propose is that organizations should become efficient in all areas of design. As some of these areas are unnecessary with some products, resources may be directed into areas where they are not required. The principle of product status ensures that financial resources, time and effort are more directly tuned into areas where they will be most beneficial.

To determine a product status two questionnaires need to be answered. Questionnaire 1 (Fig. 7.2) identifies the product status of the service in its

QUESTIONNAIRE: MACRO-PRODUCT STATUS Product type under consideration: Comparison with which product:		
Place a tick in the relevant column:	YES (Static)	NO (Dynamic)
1. If there hasn't been any technical advance recently that may be used to replace this service tick the 'Yes' column and go on to Question 6. If there has, name it and tick the 'No' column.		
2. Is there a large infrastructure based on the existing design that *cannot* be used with the new design (e.g. fuel, sales, spares, distribution, servicing, skills, etc.)? Give one tick in the 'Yes' column for each, or one tick in the 'No' column if there are none.		
3. Are there any conformance standards for this service that cannot be met by the new design?		
4. Put a tick in the 'No' column for every *two*		

advantages of the technical advance that would make a customer change from the existing service (one tick for lower price*).		
5. Put one tick in the 'Yes' column for every *two* disadvantages that would make a customer prefer the existing service.		
6. Are a few relatively large organizations dominating this service market? (Tick the 'No' column if any technical advance mentioned in Question 1 comes from one of these organizations.)		
7. Do most organizations appear to copy each other?		
8. Has the service been available in its present form for more than five years?		
9. Tick the 'Yes' column if the number of your competitors is decreasing or remaining the same. Tick the 'No' column if the number of your competitors has increased.		
10. Recently there may have been changes in the economic climate, legislation or resources that make the existing service more or less viable to consumers. Tick the 'Yes' column if these changes have made the existing service more viable or more attractive to customers. Tick the 'No' column if these changes have made the existing service less viable or less attractive to customers. (If neither leave blank.)		
TOTAL		

Results
An equal number of ticks in both columns or a surplus of ticks in the 'Yes' column indicates that the product status is probably static. A surplus of ticks in the 'No' column indicates that the product status is probably dynamic or potentially dynamic. Knowledge of this status can direct your emphasis in design.

Fig. 7.2 Questionnaire 1 — macro-product status.

current market or environment. For a new service to disturb the status quo it must be shown to be better than services already in existence. A surplus of ticks in the 'dynamic' column will be needed to indicate that the product is potentially dynamic and innovation is required.

Questionnaire 2 (Fig. 7.3) is used to find the status that prevails within

QUESTIONNAIRE: MICRO-ORGANIZATION STATUS Service name:		
Place a tick in the relevant column:	YES (Static)	NO (Dynamic)
1. Does this service interface with other services or product assemblies not made by your organization?		
*2. Do you/will you use much dedicated machinery in this service?		
*3. Do you/will you use CAD for the design of this service?		
*4. Does your organization have a greater market share or turnover than most of your competitors (or potential competitors)?		
**5. Is a fast design time one of the three most important considerations when embarking on a new design?		
**6. Must new designs use the existing sales force and/or distribution networks?		
**7. Must new designs use the existing facilities?		
**8. Must tried and proven methods be used in the design of new services?		
**9. Must new designs be an extension of the existing product range?		

10.	Is this service made by assembling components, the majority of which are made by other organizations?		
11.	Has the service design specification remained significantly unaltered recently by the market research department and by your main customers?		
12.	Do you use the same components from this service in several other services?		
	TOTAL		

*If a 'Yes' answer is given to these questions it is in your organization's interests and advantage to seek static services.
**'Yes' answers to these questions suggests that your organization is restricting design to static design. Is this necessary or sensible?

Fig. 7.3 Questionnaire 2 – micro-organization status.

your organization. By answering this questionnaire the column with the most ticks will give an indication on whether the organization is currently best organized for a static or dynamic service. There should be no mismatch between the results obtained for the two questionnaires. If the organization has a static status and the product status is dynamic then the situation in the organization needs to be adjusted to make it more suitable for a dynamic product or the market should be abandoned. If those in the organization are not prepared to alter the situation, for whatever reason, then they should concentrate on products and services that match their status.

Many services are made up of several component parts and these may contain *subinnovations*. This is more easily described by looking at manufactured products. For example, a car has over 2,000 components, which make up about 100 major subassemblies. At any one time the majority of these subassemblies are static designs, but some are dynamic. If one looks at the status of car design one can predict that a car bought in ten years' time will still have an internal combustion engine, four wheels with pneumatic tyres, a gearbox, a differential, seats, doors and a steering wheel, all of which will be very similar to those that exist at present. The innovative parts of a car are the fuel flow system, the suspension system and the braking system (but not the steering system). It is necessary to break down a large product or service into its various component parts and then identify which are changing innovatively. These are called subinnovations.

It is usually necessary to answer Questionnaire 1 for each large component or segment of the service to see if it is static or dynamic.

Product status changes, and as a result you should complete Questionnaire 1 about every six months for each service in your range to ensure that you are still treating product status in the correct fashion. An early identification of a change in product status will allow your company plenty of time to react to these changing circumstances.

Another use of the questionnaire is in competition analysis. Answer Questionnaire 2 as if you were in the position of any particular competitor. This will show if they are likely to treat their products or services as static or dynamic. Unless your competitor is actually seeking a new concept they are unlikely to find one.

The questionnaires were developed from extensive research and the factors identified that make a service static or dynamic are listed in Tables 7.1 and 7.2 respectively.

As can be seen many of the factors that make or keep a service static are, merely, the opposite of those that make or keep it dynamic. As these factors

Table 7.1 Factors that make/keep a service static

1.	Limited design time.
2.	Customers not willing to change.
3.	Stable effective service design specification.
4.	Dedicated machinery, automation, CAD, purchasing new machinery.
5.	Few large producers.
6.	Reducing or stable number of producers.
7.	Poor market research.
8.	Stable technology (product static for a long time).
9.	Market infrastructure based on existing designs.
10.	Stable/improving environment for existing design.
11.	Conformance standards.
12.	User familiarity.
13.	Restricted design (at any level, e.g. V.A.).
14.	Relying upon experience in design.
15.	Relying upon imitation in design.
16.	Restricted service design specification, (e.g. same as sales outlet, extension of existing range).
17.	Using rationalization or commonality of parts between several product components in design.
18.	Assembling components made by others.
19.	Service interfaces, or is part of, an assembly made elsewhere.
20.	Service available in its present form for a long time (static).
21.	Insufficient design/finance resources, management commitment.

Table 7.2 Factors that make/keep a service dynamic

1.	Adequate time allowed for design.
2.	Customers willing to change.
3.	Change in service design specification.
4.	Flexible machinery, subcontracting features of the service.
5.	Many small producers.
6.	Increasing number of producers.
7.	Wide effective market research (innovation seeking, market pull).
8.	Technology change.
9.	Ill-defined market infrastructure or infrastructure incapable of accepting a new design.
10.	Changing external environment (legislation, economic climate, resources).
11.	No conformance standards.
12.	Open management design guidelines.
13.	Organizations seeking new concepts.

were found from research in several specific areas we cannot be sure that the list is complete. Your organization and your markets may have different or additional factors that will affect the status. We recommend that you use the two questionnaires, but let them evolve, fine tuning them to your particular situation. Apply the questionnaires, with the benefit of hindsight, to older services, viewing these at the time they were introduced. By weighting some factors more than others a fair degree of accuracy can be obtained.

Having found the product status the important disciplines should be emphasized (or expanded). These disciplines can be divided into four broad sections.

Initially, 1., there are some that must be present with all organizations that are involved in design.

1. Services must have quality and reliability.
2. Competition analysis.
3. Innovation seeking outside of your organization.
4. Effective selling – the service must reach the customer.
5. Management commitment to design.
6. Financial control over design.
7. Effective market research.
8. Responding to market pull – the most effective trigger.

Ensure that these disciplines are in place before embarking on the design of any product or service.

The subsequent disciplines are divided into:

2. Those that should be emphasized when the service is dynamic (Table 7.3).
3. Those to be emphasized when the service is static (Table 7.4).

4.   Those to be emphasized when a service has been static for a long period of time – typically five years – static 2 status (Table 7.5).

Table 7.3 Service dynamic

Creative marketing	Technology push
Seller's market	Flexibility
Dynamic/reiterative planning	Large research effort and cost
Uncertainty/high risk/ high profit/high price	Innovation
Short product lifecycle	Labour intensive
Changing (unpredictable) environment	Customer training
Non-product-related research	Lateral flexible communication
Many competing firms	Organic design team structure

Table 7.4 Static 1: Service static

Design evolution/ service improvement	Cost reduction
Business planning	Good reputation
Emphasis on:	Fast delivery
Maintainability	Effective distribution
Low cost	Standardization
Use of standards	Capital investment
Effective purchasing	Price elasticity
CAD	Price reduction
Imitation	Mergers
After-sales service network	Increased competition
Good aesthetics	Growing vertical integration
Good ergonomics	

Table 7.5 Static 2: Service static, increasing volume,
time or (relatively) large organization

Niche marketing	'Model' changes
Low risk/low profit	Political considerations
Long product lifecycle/ short model lifecycle	Financial credit systems policy
Stable (predictable) environment	Market saturation
Specialization	Fierce competition
Rationalization	Mechanistic design team structure
Economics of scale	Number of firms declining
Automation	High capital intensity
'Just-in-Time' (Kanban)	Buyer's market
Seeking large market share	Impact on society
Technology stabilized	Synergy
Few innovations	

As many services operate with manufactured products many of these depend on the status of those manufactured products. Therefore we have provided three additional lists of disciplines that relate to manufactured products (Table 7.6).

Table 7.6 Disciplines associated with manufactured products

Dynamic status	Short production runs
	Flexible production
	Patents/design protection
	Subcontract manufacture
	Minor process design
Static status	Emphasis on:
	Finish
	Size reduction
	Assembly aids
	Group technology
	Reduction of scrap
Static 2 status	Use of different materials in design
	More process design than product design
	Long production runs/mass production
	Value analysis
	Dedicated machinery
	Robotics/FMS/CAM
	Energy conservation
	Very low cost production
	Capital intensive

Product status is relatively new, but has an important role to play in the design process. It helps to direct the subsequent emphasis in design.

Process status

A recent advancement in product design has been the consideration of carrying out aspects of the process simultaneously. This has been borrowed from the computer industry, which calls it *parallel processing*. Cooper (1988) encourages parallel processing, the main advantage being that it speeds up the process and, he believes, as there is less temptation to delete key activities it thereby maintains quality. In the manufacturing industry Duffy and Kelly (1989) call this 'simultaneous engineering', of which they say:

> [It] increases the incidence of product designs that match available resources, thereby reducing multiple redesigns. The result is a better quality product,

produced in a shorter time period with fewer changes and therefore at a lower overall development cost.

But there can be the penalty of higher management and training overheads if this is to be organized effectively.

If several aspects of a product or service design can be carried out in parallel the completed design can be made available to potential customers in less time. Parallel processing needs careful planning, usually by techniques such as critical path analysis. In theory, parallel processing must be a good idea. If the whole design process could be concertinaed into less time the product could reach the market ahead of the competition and there would be less time for markets or environments to change. In practice, parallel processing is not that easy. It can work well if the design is static and those involved are familiar with the techniques that will be involved. With dynamic designs the design team cannot rely on experience – they are dealing with something new. As a result, in this situation, parallel processing can cause problems. This is because it is difficult to anticipate the time taken to do something new and, therefore, difficult to draw up an accurate programme schedule.

Product status will identify whether the design concepts are to be new or those already existing will suffice. Innovation takes longer, which must be allowed for in the programme. As an extra dimension to parallel processing we have found, in our consultancy, that it is useful to evaluate the process status. With process status it is only necessary to consider what is a new process to your organization. By identifying these new processes, more time can be given to them in the design. If a process is new to your organization, or your existing subcontractors, but already well known elsewhere, it will still take longer for you to become familiar with it. Typically, an additional 10 per cent time penalty must be added to such processes in your programme schedule. If the process is absolutely new, but within your existing capabilities, then it will take much longer, perhaps twice as long as something you have dealt with previously. The important statement here is 'within your existing capabilities'. It will take twice as long if you have the technology and the trained personnel available. If you do not have these it could take even longer and you should think again before embarking on projects in such areas.

All this requires a *service audit*. This is a listing of all your current capabilities as well as the capabilities of your usual suppliers, subcontractors and distributors. With this listing it is possible to state that your organization can treat these aspects of the design as a static process or a dynamic process. If your design is made up of static processes then parallel processing can be recommended. If aspects of the design contain dynamic processes then these must be given a priority.

Therefore, in most new service designs there are likely to be some processes which are static and some dynamic. Those dynamic processes must be started first and they require a greater degree of testing to ensure reliability. There will come a time, part way through the design of these dynamic processes, where there is sufficient confidence to be sure of a successful completion within a certain time. At this stage the design of the static processes can start simultaneously and parallel processing will continue throughout the subsequent stages of the process.

This is shown, simply, in Fig. 7.4. Process status does enable one to identify difficult and slower areas of the process. These areas are to be given priority with extra manpower and resources directed towards them. The subsequent stages can then be compacted through parallel processing.

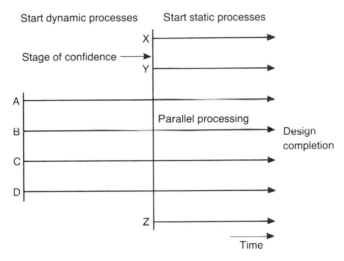

Fig. 7.4 Parallel processing of dynamic and static processes.

The service audit, of course, is not dependent on any particular product and once it has been compiled it can be used for each new design. As every design is completed, those dynamic processes which are completed thus become static processes and these are added to the service audit. The service audit will build, over the years, as the organization becomes more experienced in wider areas. Sometimes areas of expertise will need to be deleted from the audit as certain people leave or distributors, suppliers and subcontractors change.

The service audit takes some time to compile – typically four man-weeks in a small to medium organization – and should, therefore, be carried out at 'quieter' times in the design calender.

========== **Summary** ==========

• An innovation is an invention in its first marketable form. Most new products are not innovations. An innovation takes longer, costs more, is more difficult and has a higher risk of failure than an incremental change. Innovation is not necessary with most designs and should be avoided. When innovation is required an organization must do so otherwise it will be left behind by the competition.

- The need for innovation (dynamic design) or incremental change (static design) can be identified through answering the product status questionnaires.

- When the product status has been found various design activities or 'disciplines' should be accentuated or diminished depending on the product status. Product status, therefore, simplifies the design process.

- Process status relates to areas of experience that exist within an organization or their main suppliers. By identifying the process status, through a service audit, it is possible to 'compress' the design process by the introduction of parallel processing. In this, dynamic process design will be given a priority over static process design. When the new process is sufficiently understood dynamic and static processes can be undertaken in parallel.

Chapter 8

The early stages of
service design in detail

Earlier we described the basic stages of the design process. This chapter is for the practitioner who will actually be designing services, so we now describe the early stages of this process more fully.

Cowell (1984) suggests that, 'While the terminology of new product development and the range and order of steps included in the process varies, the underlying notions behind the use of systematic procedures does not.' Here the design process is broken down into a workable sequence identified through our research and consultancy which should be followed. When designing products or services be certain that, at any stage of the design, (1) the objectives are clearly defined and (2) the roles and responsibilities are understood.

The process we describe takes a layered approach. The activities proposed at each layer should be completed before proceeding to the next layer of the design process.

The key to the process is the use of subspecifications that are compiled at specified points in the early, low-cost, stages of the design. The information gathered for each of these subspecifications is increased and refined at each layer. Eventually these subspecifications build into the full service design specification (SDS). This gradual building of information, coupled with continuous assessment of the design aims, avoids the large input of work that could occur if one complete SDS was written directly after the marketing stage. If compromises could not be reached in the SDS the design would be abandoned and a lot of effort wasted. The gradual build-up through subspecifications allows a degree of 'dipping one's toes in the water before taking the plunge'.

Endeavour to make as many of the design decisions at the low-cost end of the design process. These decisions should be taken whilst the design is still in a paper or very simple prototype form. This will allow designs to be severely modified, or abandoned, without incurring significant expense. Cooper (1983, 1988), who has done more than most to investigate a suitable structure for the design process, emphasizes the need for 'doing it right first time' rather than

117

having to backtrack and rework key steps. He suggests that more time and resources must be devoted to the activities preceding the development of a product. Initial screening, analysis and definition of stages all constitute critical steps to success. This will also reduce the time taken for a design to reach the market – very important in today's reducing service and product lifecycles.

Subspecifications are compiled by various groups, some prior to the formation of the design circle. Some of these early subspecifications provide a boundary round the proposed service and parameters to which all the proposed services must conform. These include the main management guidelines and the skills audit, which are applicable to many services the organization may wish to design. This means that it will become immediately obvious that certain services are unsuitable for an organization and these service ideas can be abandoned before hardly any investment has been made. Other subspecifications will be particular to the proposed new service. 'Gaps' in the design knowledge will also be identified – these should be filled before proceeding to the next stage of the process.

At first sight it could appear that organizations are being advised to be 'production orientated' rather than 'market orientated' as is generally proposed (e.g. Kotler (1986, 1988), who has written several books on marketing, has advised this market orientation). In certain cases it is necessary to accept that some organizations would be ill advised to invest in areas where they do not have the finance, plant, distribution, suitable environment or expertise available. Furthermore, in such cases, it would not be worthwhile embarking on making these available.

As each subspecification limits the potential scope of the design, care must be taken not to define the acceptable areas so tightly that subsequent innovation or 'flair' is stifled.

The various subspecifications are combined to make the full SDS in the eighth layer of the process. This will be co-ordinated by the product champion, who will be one of the few people to have the entire document. He will be responsible for ensuring that there are no contradictions between these subspecifications, but, where they do occur, he will call together the parties who drew up the conflicting subspecifications to achieve a compromise on those most important elements that make up the SDS. The entire design plan is shown, in its basic form later in Fig. 8.1.

In this chapter we only describe what should be done and when it should be done in the early stages of the design process. To see how these early stages could be applied in practice, in Chapter 13 we provide a worked example of the system in which we show how the stages are used with a typical service design.

At each stage of this process there is a 'bail out' point, similar to that proposed by Cooper (1983), where the service design is assessed. Here a decision is taken to proceed, iterate the design project back to the screening stage, or abandon the design. Bearing in mind the high failure rate of new products and services and the geometric rise in product development costs the further one gets into the design process, the earlier one can identify a potential failure, abandon it and get on with designing something potentially more successful, the better it will be for the organization in terms of cost, time and lost opportunity.

Compiling these subspecifications indicates not only the close co-operation between those who are in the various roles that have traditionally been thought of as 'design', but also, more importantly, other people as well. This demonstrates the need for truly multidisciplinary design – which is the hallmark of Total Design.

Various people will be responsible for the implementation of these stages and they should have this responsibility included as part of their job description. This should also indicate where additional training must be given to enable those involved to do these tasks.

The design methodology, as described, takes a 'top to bottom' approach but will, in practice, be iterative. Iteration is important throughout the design process. If further information is required on any stage of design, then go back (or forward) to retrieve this information. This could be the introduction of a new service by a competitor or a change in some aspect of the market. The most up-to-date and improved information must be considered whenever it becomes available. This can, in some circumstances, even indicate the discontinuation of the design. This means that, as new and better information becomes available, those involved in the process may need to backtrack to check on or change some of the earlier work. There comes a point where further changes are unnecessarily disruptive, time consuming and expensive. This control of iteration at the later stages of the design process is also a sign of good design management.

Select a leader

It is unlikely that an organization in the service sector will have someone who has the clearly defined role of design director. There are, however, exceptions to this, such as British Rail. Before a company can embark on a new service product programme someone should be appointed to head the design function. The appointment must be at a senior level if new products and services are to be taken seriously by the organization. The person chosen to be leader of the design function must have sufficient authority to be able to make important decisions. In this chapter we refer to him as the design director, because anybody who is in charge of design should be of board level. This person may also be the product champion, but, where several services are being developed at the same time in an organization, there will be a product champion – or design manager – heading up each design process. These individual design managers will, of course, report to the design director.

Layer 1: Main management guidelines

The board must state the 'main management guidelines', which are broad parameters to which any new service or product must conform and limitations to what may be designed. Sidney Gregory who was writing and thinking about design management many years ago considered that this was an area of importance. He emphasized in Langdon and Rothwell (1987) the need for clear, explicit policy directives from top management to provide an acceptable basis for the evaluation of proposals and then went on to suggest an 'ethical code' for designers, which promotes inter-disciplinary skills in the design function. The commitment and involvement of top management in design strategy is of vital importance, as it impinges on product strategy and hence overall corporate strategy.

In an article Christopher Parkes (1989) refers to a report by GAH, a London-based consultancy, which found several main management deficiencies in product development in Britain, which included:

1. Top management take little interest in product development.
2. Few companies integrate new product development into their overall business strategy. The resulting products may occasionally be individually successful. They are, however, unlikely to provide the ideal fit with the company's overall business strategy.
3. Lack of effective direction from the top. In most companies product development is at the whim of managers. They do it because it takes their fancy but not necessarily because it is attractive to the company itself.
4. This leads to a project-by-project approach instead of an integrated portfolio. Processing ideas simply leads to the situation where top management become involved only when a project is at a stage where requests have to be made for funds and senior people to make their evaluation – usually on strict financial grounds – and either bring the project to a dead stop or send it forward to an uncertain future.
5. There is a failure to assess total new product development investment in terms of management time and hard cash.

Financial control over the design process is one of the main areas of importance in design management. At this stage the financial limitations should be fairly clearly defined. From this it is often apparent if it will be possible to complete the design process before much work or investment has been made on the design. Any doubt in this area should be clarified after the product definition stage. As Leech and Turner (1985) have said, 'At a very early stage in the life of any project, the designer must do enough work to forecast the costs which will be incurred.' Therefore, before embarking on the design of any product, the top management must ensure that:

1.   They have financial control over the design process.
2.   The new product will fit in with the overall business strategy.

Furthermore, it is also essential that certain disciplines are in place so that the organization can cope with and benefit from the design effort. They should ensure the following mechanisms in the organization:

1.   Systems to guarantee quality and reliability.
2.   Effectiveness at reacting to market pull.
3.   An effective sales unit.

Generally the main management guidelines place boundaries around various organizational activities which restrict the designer's freedom. For example, Alan Cane (1990) says, 'Managing Director's attitude towards technology usually determines how effectively a company deploys its technological effort.'

The main management guidelines should be presented in the first of a series of subspecifications. These should cover areas determined from the questionnaire outlined in Table 8.1, which top management (directors) should consider before investigating a new series of design projects.

Table 8.1   Main management guidelines questionnaire

For the design to be right for your organization must the new service:
1.   Use the existing form of distribution?
2.   Be produced by your organization?
3.   Meet some specified volume or demand?
4.   Meet some specified minimum profit margin?
5.   Reach a minimum turnover?
6.   Have a maximum payback period?
7.   Be an extension of the existing product/service range?
8.   Have a maximum design timescale?
9.   Have a specific maximum commitment in management time?
10.   Use, or avoid using, certain areas of technology?
11.   Have synergy with existing products and services in the organization?

More guidelines may be added as suits your organization. The more precise one can make these main management guidelines the less likely there is to be confusion in aims. It is also more likely that people will work within these clearly defined parameters.

It must be remembered that specifying a tight timescale for completing any project will limit the degree of innovation possible. In such circumstances, those involved in the subsequent stages of the design will be forced to rely more on experience and tried and tested methods.

Having identified and specified the main management guidelines those involved in new products will then avoid developing services that do not meet the aims and objectives of the organization. These main management guidelines will almost certainly apply to all services being designed in the organization.

Now the design circle should be formed by the design director. This should include all those who can contribute to the areas of the design that require initial consideration. Individuals in the design circle will undertake aspects of the design and then the design circle will meet to ensure that the requirement of the subspecification has been met. The design circle will also be responsible for compiling most of these subspecifications. At certain specified key stages of the design process there will be a main design review where a decision will be taken to:

1. Continue the design;
2. 'Hold' the design and iterate back to an earlier stage in the process to update or clarify the information; or,
3. Abandon the design.

Layer 2: The strategic specification and initial market input

The following two subspecifications can be compiled in parallel.

The strategic specification

It is necessary to define the objective of the service to be designed as part of your strategic plan. At the most senior level, management must endeavour to identify where they require the organization's services to be at specified points in time. This information should be precise. Present this in the form of a document and include tolerances on the information supplied.

All organizations have a strategic product plan and this may provide the input to this specification. Typically, though, organizations word their strategies in language, such as 'to deliver, on time, a superior quality product at the lowest possible cost, whatever the volume the customer wants'. This is far too vague and such strategies have been described by Les Galloway, who lectures in Operations Management at Leicester Polytechnic, as 'impossible dreams and not to be taken seriously'.

Although the Board of Directors may be in control of their business they are often inaccurate in their assessment of their market needs (Hollins 1978). This is because they are not usually in daily contact with their market. If the strategic specification describes a precise programme for a new service it is likely to be altered, significantly, by the marketing department, who have better information on which to base their decisions. Certain aspects of the strategic plan may be fixed (e.g. the main purpose of the service) and these should be specified.

The strategic specification should contain well defined, specific goals that people can work towards. The personnel involved in compiling this specification will be directors and senior management in finance, marketing and design.

A proposed outline of a strategic specification service form is shown in Table 8.2. This document will have no specific length, but the more parameters that can be given at this stage the better – under 1,500 words is insufficient to give clear guidelines. This should be supplied to the product champion, and it must be accepted that the task of acquiring information not included on the form will be delegated to the various experts in the organization by him. The parts to be included in the strategic specification will vary, depending on the particular requirements of your service. Through our consultancy work we have found that Table 8.2 covers many of the important points that need consideration at this stage of the design process. (As an exercise, which of these items must not be altered in the subsequent stages of design without direct approval of the board?)

Table 8.2 Strategic specification for services

1.	Name of service to be designed.
2.	New service or update of existing service.
3.	Trigger for the new service.
4.	Description of new service.
5.	Main purpose of the service.
6.	Features to be included (wants and needs?).
7.	Reason why the new service is required. (This can be to satisfy an identified demand, to fill spare capacity, as a defence against competition, etc.)
*8.	Quantity to be produced in the first year, second year and third year of production.
*9.	Cost to provide (including an estimation of overheads).
10.	Maximum timescale for completion up to the point of delivery to the first customers.
12.	Financial return expected.
13.	Other financial limitations.
14.	Resources to be devoted to the design (production, marketing, testing, etc.)
15.	Priority against other design projects.
16.	Availability of appropriate personnel.

*Place a tolerance on items 8 and 9.

Initial market input

Design must be market led because not understanding the requirements of customers is the main reason for design failures. It has also been shown that the most successful 'trigger' for new products is market pull. Therefore, finding out what potential customers require, for the next generation of services, is vital.

At the early stage of design a very broad list of product requirements should be drawn up. Much of this information can be found from desk research coupled with marketing research of existing and potential customers. These requirements will be refined at a later stage in the design process, but at this stage all that is necessary is a broad outline of market need. Table 8.3 shows the initial marketing specification elements put in the form of a simple questionnaire. Much of this can be answered by existing and potential customers and other parts by people within the organization.

Table 8.3 Initial marketing specification questionnaire

Name of potential new service:

1.	Who will use the service?
2.	How will it reach potential customers?
3.	What is the market size, how many customers per year?
4.	At what price will it be sold?
5.	How often will it be purchased?
6.	Is it a fashion or 'gimmick' type item?
7.	How will customers get to hear of it?
8.	How will the service be used?
9.	What type of people will buy it?
10.	What type of demand pattern will there be: daily, weekly, yearly?
11.	What is the level of potential competition?
12.	How will the service product be better than the competition?
13.	How can it be further improved?

Preferably this questionnaire should be delivered and completed face to face to facilitate easier discussion and to identify suitable areas of compromise. The marketing department will be responsible for collecting and compiling this information. The questionnaire should seek quantitative answers where possible and these answers should include tolerances (the range of acceptability). This is the third main input into the design methodology and should essentially answer the question: 'Why will they buy (or will not buy) our service?'

The answers to these questions, at this stage, are bound to be fairly basic. They will include some educated guesses as well as some 'order of magnitude' type answers. Do not seek the information from outside of your organization if it can be obtained by desk research, by asking the various experts that already exist in-house, or by using other systems that can be set up. For example, are customer complaints collected and possible design faults identified from them? If not, introduce a monitoring system, complete with a questionnaire, to discuss product problems with customers as quickly as possible.

The results of the questionnaire should be compiled into the initial marketing specification. A copy must be circulated to all those who provided an input into it to enable them to comment on the interpretation of their analysis of the market.

Be aware that the answers to the questions given in Table 8.3 may well indicate a customer requirement for a service that is already in your range, thus avoiding the need to design a new service.

Table 8.4 Feedback questionnaire

Plese complete and return. Continue oversheet if necessary.

1. Was my report an accurate description of what you said?
2. Was my report an accurate description of the situation that exists in your company?
3. Is our list of your service requirements accurate? (If 'no' please state the inaccuracies.)
4. Was the report helpful in giving you an understanding of the type of service you need? (If 'no' please state ways in which it could be improved.)
5. How can we improve the accuracy of this market research?
6. Will the conclusions and recommendations for the service, if followed, provide a service suited to your requirements?
7. Are there any additional features that you would like incorporated into the product?
8. Please indicate which of these additional features are absolutely essential to your requirements and how much extra you would be prepared to pay each one.

Thank you for completing this questionnaire. We hope that this enables us to supply a service better suited to your needs.

Table 8.4 shows a feedback questionnaire that, where possible, should be given to confirm the accuracy of the initial marketing specification compiled from the initial marketing specification questionnaire. This is a development of an earlier questionnaire that has been successfully used to determine the accuracy in interpretation of some of our research data collected by questionnaire. For those who are not in your organization this feedback questionnaire can be done entirely through the post, or, preferably, after sending it through the post, the questions can then be discussed by telephone. This is only possible if the potential customers for the new service are already known to you. In most cases, and for most markets, it will not be possible to administer this feedback questionnaire.

A main design review should now be held at this stage of the design process.

Layer 3: Relevant innovations and competition analysis

The next two stages can also be carried out in parallel.

Relevant innovations

The fourth main input is the identification of possible new innovations that are likely to affect your market. These may be threats of new potential competition, but such threats can be identified early enough to be opportunities from which your organization can benefit. This function is not necessarily product related and should be an ongoing process, carried out by those in your design department.

The economist Burton Klein (1977) and Jewkes *et al.* (1969), writers on innovation, have shown that many major innovations are not pioneered by those organizations currently involved in a market, but are most likely to emanate from other organizations. Other work (Hollins and Pugh 1990) has shown that there is sufficient time, in most cases, for an organization to identify such potential threats and act in their best interests to benefit from these changes. This is providing that they are seeking these innovations by reading scientific and technical journals and visiting exhibitions and conferences, other than those which are more obviously concerned with their market and organizational activities.

It is considered that one person, limited to one day each month, is sufficient to do this 'innovation seeking'. Seniority is not important for this function, but a lively mind is necessary to be able to 'read across' these changes occurring in universities and other market sectors which can be applied in your own organization. The person assigned to this job must provide a report for the main design circle every three months, proposing various possible ideas and how they could relate to existing or new organizational activities. An ability to relate to new inventions is the necessary skill.

Competition analysis

The fifth input into the early stages of design will be competition analysis. This will take the form of desk research, undertaken in the design department. Again, seniority is unimportant. The purpose is to determine what the direct competition is currently doing and to identify trends that may indicate the direction of design in the future and, perhaps, identify the important aspects of design.

You will certainly know the most obvious competitors in your product market and you should draw up a dossier on each one, based on Table 8.5. These dossiers will state market position and the strengths and weaknesses of each product. The strengths may be copied and their weaknesses may be used to gain a marketing advantage.

Table 8.5 Competitor's dossier

The name of the organization.
Size (turnover, number of employees involved in the product under consideration).
Address of all main centres.
Country and city of agents.
Percentage of competing market.
Service product A: (name).
    Strengths (technical and market).
    Weaknesses (technical and market).
Service features, advantages and disadvantages, pricing.
In what areas are they innovative?

Most of this information will be obtained from their catalogues, or by discreet discussions with their sales personnel at trade exhibitions. Much of it can also provide the inputs to parametric analysis.

To determine if the competition is innovative the status questionnaire can be used. Take the role of the competitor and answer the questions as if you were they. Fundamentally, if the organization is not actually seeking new innovations then their products will remain static designs and they will only progress by following more innovative organizations.

Layer 4: Screening

The threads, thus far, are drawn together into a feasibility study at the product screening stage. This is basically just another design review, but it has a special purpose. Here the design circle will endeavour to reach a compromise between the various subspecifications. The information collected will indicate the new potential products or services with initial costings and these areas of design will then be defined. This is a key point in the design process as decisions made here will involve considerable subsequent involvement in time and resources.

The screening stage is also the only point where the decision is taken to abandon a design project. If a product fails to meet the various subspecifications at any point in the design process, it will be iterated back to the previous stages for correction or adaptation of the relevant subspecification. If there can be no compromise in the design or specification, which means that the design will result in a failed product, service or process, it will be abandoned.

The design will be iterated back, stage by stage, until it reaches the product screening stages and here it can be abandoned. This will not take as long as it would first appear.

This decision will be taken by the most senior members of the design circle, but is the responsibility of the product champion.

127

Service product definition

From the information so far compiled (mainly from the market), it will become obvious if there is to be one or several products to be designed. It will also be obvious which will have the highest priority. These service products must now be defined so that all those involved in the design process are aware of the forthcoming service and all have the same understanding of what the new service is intended to be. The service product definition should be the outcome of the *screening*.

Defining *precisely* what the service is to be will enable you to state what the competition is and at what market the service is to be aimed. This will also allow one to focus on the information that needs to be collected from which the product status can later be found.

The service product definition may be very narrow, and if it is defined too narrowly, it may be conceptually vulnerable. If at the concept stage it is shown not to be conceptually vulnerable the subsequent design process will be easier. Table 8.6 lists the items to be found in the service product definition.

Table 8.6 The service product definition

1.	The service title.
2.	What purpose the service is to perform.
3.	Against what type of service it will be competing.
4.	What market it will serve. Who will buy/use the service and when will it be used?
5.	The anticipated performance parameters.
6.	Who are the competitors?
7.	Why is there a need and what are the customer benefits?
8.	The anticipated demand/selling price.
9.	The cost at that demand.
10.	Who are the customers?
11.	How will the service reach the customers (promotion and distribution)?
12.	How will it be used (including demand patterns)?
13.	Can it, will it, replace an existing service?

Fifteen hundred words should be the minimum length of the service product definition. Significantly more than this probably isn't necessary, as it is only a description from which the design process (but not the design) can proceed.

Educated guesses can be allowed (for example, anticipated demand and price) as, even though these are likely to be inaccurate, they will be an aid to the understanding of the service design under consideration and will lay the foundation for the information which will be refined and expanded in subsequent stages of the design methodology.

══════ **Layer 5: Product status specification** ══════

A product status specification is a short written document compiled after an investigation into certain aspects of the service. From this the status questionnaires (macro and micro – *see* Figs 7.2 and 7.3) can be answered so that the product status can be found. Product status indicates if innovation is, or is not, required.

The factors to be considered in compiling the product status specification are listed in Table 8.7. The depth of investigation need only be sufficient to answer the status questionnaires with confidence.

Table 8.7 Factors in compiling the product status specification

1.	Competition analysis:	– Pricing/quantity – Number and size of competitors (quantity) – Product features, advantages and disadvantages
2.	Market research:	– Relevant legislation – Relevant economic information – Relevant resources – Relevant standards – Infrastructure around current service, e.g. fuel, spares, maintenance, distribution, selling skills, etc.
3.	Innovation seeking outside of your industry:	– Technical changes that may be used in your design or be a threat to the concept, product, or market

The *service audit* states, in broad terms, the existing capabilities of the organization and their main sub-contractors. The audit will be used to identify the known and available experience or 'production' know-how (*see* page 114). The service audit is not part of the design of a particular service but the information included in it is required. The service audit can be compiled and updated on a continuous basis. Initially it will take some weeks to compile but updating will only take one person about half of one day each month. The product champion should arrange for the service audit to be available for inspection at the start of Layer 6 in the design process.

══════ **Layer 6: Preliminary technical specification** ══════

With a knowledge of the product status the preliminary technical specification can then be drawn up. This will be undertaken by members of the process/production or implementation departments, including an industrial designer (if it is to be that type of service), under the leadership of the product champion. The content of this subspecification will vary depending on the earlier information obtained but is likely to include the elements in Table 8.8.

Table 8.8 Elements of the preliminary technical specification

Safety
Legal
Insurance
Conformance standards
Quality and reliability
Maintenance/servicing and service facility required
Anticipated service costings refined
Timescale for the product to be launched
Testing
Life in service
Ergonomics
Aesthetics
Pollution
Disposal
Processes
Materials
Energy requirements/consumption
Skills/human resources

Preliminary marketing specification

A preliminary marketing specification will also be required at this stage and this will be assembled by the marketing department. This is compiled at the same time as the preliminary technical specification. As compromises are needed between these two specifications it will be necessary for those with the differing interests to work closely together. Table 8.9 shows the areas that should be confronted in this subspecification.

Table 8.9 Preliminary marketing specification

Performance features
Market constraints
Shipping/effective distribution/service facility
Presentation
Communication
Availability
User standards – custom and practice
Image
Competition
Service sales price/quantity

Service lifespan (period it will be on sale)
Customer training
Politics — relevant government policy
Preliminary marketing strategy (e.g. promotion)
Potential for expansion

It is at this stage of the design process where the various subspecifications are compiled into the service design specification (SDS). This will also include additional elements that have not yet been considered.

Design plan

There are now sufficient inputs to the early stages of the design process to be able to produce a rigid structure for the first part of the design process. This is shown in Fig. 8.1.

Initially, there are the main management guidelines that specify what is to be allowed, or included, in design.

The strategic input, marketing desk research and the marketing input should be supplied in parallel and a compromise reached between them before progressing further.

The input from the competition analysis and relevant recent innovations will then be considered, which will help shape the type of product(s) to be designed.

Meetings of the design circle will have been held at each of these stages to ensure that all who can make a contribution will have done so, but the first major design review will be held at the screening stage, to confirm the continuance of the various design programmes and to establish priorities.

The product definitions for each discrete service design will then be written. The product having been defined, the next stage is to determine its status, so that the important likely disciplines can be specified. This will also give an indication of the time required to complete the design process as innovation takes longer.

The service audit will then come into play to identify which areas are 'known' and which may require additional understanding.

The preliminary technical specification and marketing specification, at the next stage, can be compiled with the knowledge of the product status and service audit and, therefore, some elements will be clearly unimportant.

The full service design specification can then be compiled from the various subspecifications and will be followed by the concept and detail stages of design. The *concept stage* will be better focused in the light of the product status; if certain aspects of the service are static there will be no need to seek new concepts for them and the existing concepts will suffice. Knowing the areas where innovation is required will then enable these parts of the product, and subsequently the

131

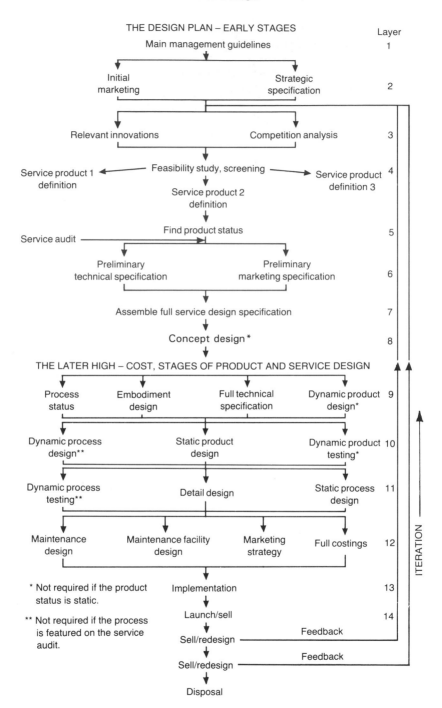

Fig. 8.1 The design plan.

process, to be given a degree of priority ahead of those where experience can be used. The known areas can be designed using parallel processing.

During the later, high cost, stages of the design process the serious expenditure begins. Up to this stage the design work has been presented in the form of written documents. Although this documentation will continue it will be supplemented by more detailed work including prototyping, testing, purchasing and construction.

The main management decisions will have been made by this stage and the emphasis in the design process will subsequently be directed towards fine tuning and implementing these decisions. This does not mean that the subsequent stages are easy – there is a lot of truth in the expression 'the devil's in the detail'. The later stages are mainly undertaken by specialists and the management function here is to co-ordinate and orchestrate these specialisms. Often, this can be controlled and organized in a mechanistic form of communication, as if in the form of a subcontract.

If the product status is static and, therefore, the existing concept is satisfactory, dynamic product design and testing will not be required. Likewise, if there is already experience in the organization of a particular process and it appears on the service audit, the dynamic process design and testing can be omitted from the design process.

'Embodiment design' was first termed by Ken Wallace (1984) (in Pahl and Beitz 1984) and is a holistic presentation of the design. The usual form for this is a general arrangement drawing or layout that outlines the major elements of the design.

Although parallel processing achieves faster design, it is more successful when used in areas where experience can be used. For this reason those 'unknown' aspects of design – the dynamic product and process design and testing – are given a priority in the process. When the design of these has reached the stage where they are understood and risk of failure has been eliminated, they can then be undertaken in parallel processing with the more familiar (static) aspects of the design.

Throughout the later stages of the design process there must be a constant reappraisal of the costs, both for the design process and of the eventual service product. If these costs rise faster than anticipated an immediate 'hold' should be placed on the project to investigate where these increases have occurred and what has caused them.

All the foregoing work is put into practice at the implementation stage. The main financial investment occurs here but if the earlier stages have been correctly completed then the risk of failure should be low.

Summary

- The design process can be broken down into workable stages. The key to this is the use of subspecifications, which should be compiled at certain points in the early, low-cost stage of the design. This is when many of the management design decisions should be made, i.e. to proceed, iterate back or abandon the design.

- Subspecifications are compiled by various groups, who are co-ordinated and led by the product champion.

- The process takes a layered approach. Some parts can be carried out in parallel and iteration can occur, although each layer must be completed before moving on to the next layer.

- Where compromises cannot be met between subspecifications, the process should be iterated back to the previous layer. If a solution cannot be found the design project should be iterated back to the screening stage where it may be abandoned.

Who does it?

Chapter 9

Design teams

Design circles

Design is a multidisciplinary activity and one person must be the kingpin. This person will be responsible for ensuring that communication is effective, that the design process is well co-ordinated and also that the right decisions are taken. We will show that this is the 'product champion' who leads the design team. In Total Design, as there are so many factors that need to be constantly reviewed, a good product champion must be the 'master juggler'.

Being a team effort everybody who can make a contribution to the improvement of the service should be involved, but this, in itself, can cause problems. Design teams can get too big to function efficiently. They become difficult to organize and communication breaks down. In Fig. 9.1 Barry Dagger of the Engineering Industries Training Board shows what can happen if communication breaks down in a company trying to design products.

Clearly, if everybody who ought to be involved is to be heard, a system needs to be devised so that this can happen. We have found that such a system is the 'design circle'.

Burns and Stalker (1961) of Edinburgh University investigated the effects of new technology in the electronics industry in Scotland and compared this with more traditional industries. They found that the organic form of communication was more effective when change is occurring in organizations. This finding has been confirmed in many subsequent studies. For example, Herriot (1984), the Design Council (1985), Johne and Snelson (1988), and Takeuchi and Nanaka (1986) have all recently confirmed the effectiveness of the organic system during times of organizational change.

The organic system has a more 'lateral' type of communication and, as Burns and Stalker put it, 'tends to resemble lateral consultation rather than vertical command'. James Pilditch has commented on this by saying, 'designers do it horizontally!'

The opposite is a 'mechanistic' system where problems can be broken down into a series of specialisms 'as if it were the subject of a subcontract', (Burns

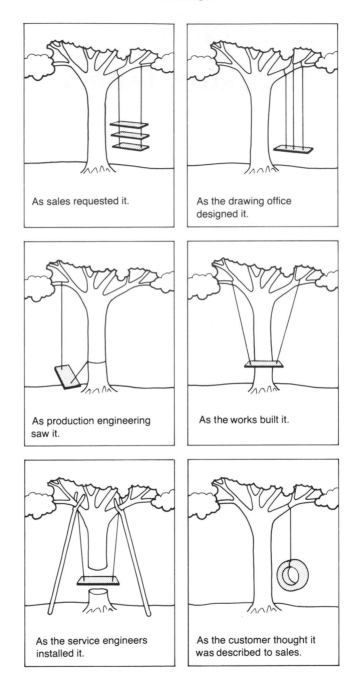

Fig. 9.1 How *not* to design a swing! Conflicting aims come from different parts of the organization.
(Source: Barry Dagger, EITB.)

and Stalker 1961). In this, direction is by formal rules and is typically shown by a pyramid type of communication and organizational chart.

In 1962 Professor Kaora Ishikawa developed the idea of the 'quality circle' in the Nippon Telegraph and Cable Company of Japan (*see The Guardian*, 17 April, 1989). Quality circles have been defined as 'small groups of employees who meet regularly to solve problems and find ways of improving aspects of their work' (Institute of Quality Assurance). This was found to be very successful and by 1978 there were one million quality circles in Japan involving some 10 million workers. Today there are reckoned to be twice that number, although, as we shall see later in this chapter, these figures suggest that the average size of a Japanese quality circle is, perhaps, too large to be altogether efficient. The quality circle, however, promotes the organic form of communication found to be so effective when change is occurring.

This idea was taken a stage further by Mark Oakley (1984) of Aston University who, when discussing the way to undertake design reviews stated:

> The most effective way is often to use small groups of employees drawn from different parts of the company to evaluate products and designs. For some time this approach has been increasingly used with success to tackle manufacturing problems – readers will be familiar with the term 'Quality Circle' often used to describe this group activity. There is no reason why 'Design Circles' should not operate in the same manner and, in fact, they have been for many years, but they are usually called value analysis groups. (Page 123.)

We have found that design circles really do work to improve communication and to facilitate decision-making, not just when the design is established but much earlier. The design circle can work from the market research stage through the whole design process. Of course not everybody who would be involved at some time or another would be included every time. The personnel in the design circle will change as the various stages of the design process are completed. New faces will join and others will leave, perhaps, to rejoin at a later stage as their particular expertise again becomes relevant. This is shown in Fig. 9.2.

Membership of the design circle is, therefore, fluid and will include those best suited to meet the objectives, which are to progress the design to the next stage of the process. This may even include outside consultants if a particular necessary expertise is not available in the company, although consultants tend to be expensive and are more effective after the SDS has been written. As the design progresses through the various stages of the process the design circle will develop until it could eventually be transformed into a quality circle when the service has been implemented and is established on the market.

The design circle gives an opportunity for those with a different expertise and background to meet on an equal footing, an essential factor as Lovelock (1988) has stated: 'Conflict occurs when power is unevenly distributed among participants, each of whom has its own perspective and agenda.'

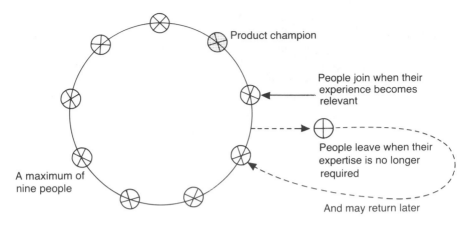

Fig. 9.2 The design circle.

We have previously touched on the lack of communication between people from different occupations. Especially in large companies, people quite often do not understand what someone else does. They do not know what information the other needs to do his job, and they do not understand how one person's decisions can affect the work done by others. Design circles help to alleviate all of these problems. At times it is advisable to include a customer in the design circle, especially if this customer will be purchasing a significant amount of the new service.

With more people being involved in the decision-making process the better these decisions are likely to be, up to a point. That point, or rather the maximum size of the group, has been determined by the occupational psychologist Edgar Schein (1969) as nine or under. Above nine the group tends to break down into subgroups and communication generally is less effective. So the maximum size of the design circle should be nine at any one meeting.

Occasionally in the design process the number of people who can make a relevant input exceeds nine. When this occurs two design circles should be formed, operating in parallel. This should only be for a short period and as soon as possible the circles must be merged into a single design circle again. With some large design projects it may be necessary to organize the people side of the design process as shown in Fig. 9.3. This means that the people in the outside circle do not have a direct say in the decision-making process. But at least the situation is more 'organic' and they are closer to the main hub than would be the case in a more normal pyramid type of communication system. We don't profess that this is perfect but it is the best that we have been able to devise.

It will be noticed that as the design progresses through the various stages of the process the seniority of the members will reduce. At the beginning the design circle may include several directors or very senior managers when

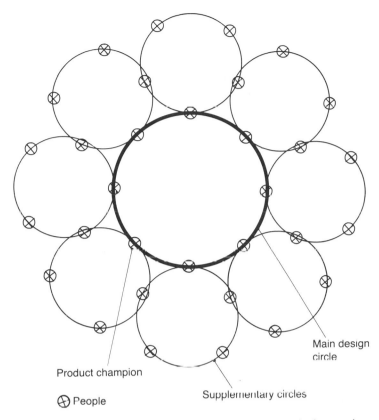

Main design circle

Product champion

Supplementary circles

⊕ People

Fig. 9.3 Organization of design circles for a large design project.

management and financial commitment to the subsequent product is being discussed. Further along the process departmental heads will make up the majority of the group and this will progress until, at the quality circle stage, the group is made up mainly of direct operatives. This is only a general rule of thumb and, if the input of the managing director is essential part way through the project, he should be invited to attend.

At the concept stage, the design circle makes an excellent brainstorming group. People's diverse backgrounds and expertise, and the number of members in the group, will help with the creative process. The ideas that emerge from this brainstorming will subsequently be refined after reference to the SDS.

One of the certain things a design manager knows about his working world is that it will change. Design, by its very nature, involves constant change and, therefore, it would appear that an organic system should be proposed throughout. This is generally the case and the design circle encourages this lateral communication found to be effective, especially in innovation. Of course, this communication must be allowed to flourish and individuals should not be able to 'pull rank'. In practice, of course, this is bound to happen occasionally because the most senior people often have their hands on better information covering wider aspects of the company organization and strategy. Apart from being more effective, the organic system has also been found to be more popular with those having to use it (Fullan 1970).

The mechanistic system, therefore, may not be suitable in most design situations, but does become more effective at the later stages of Total Design. At these later stages of the design process much of the work involves specialists and those tasks really can be operated in the organization as a series of subcontracts. Each discipline is then operated as a separate 'cell', receiving an input and processing it to produce an output. Furthermore, the mechanistic form of organization is easier to control, when change is limited, but otherwise it is less effective than the organic form.

A lot of commentators propose that mechanistic communication should be brought in much earlier, after the creative stages and before the design is implemented. As the organic system seems to work in quality circles and value analysis groups, we think it would aid decision-making in almost all areas. This includes when the design is in the early stages of implementation, especially if it is dynamic.

Using a design circle allows for an organic design team structure, even in a large organization, with the benefits of improved communication which, up to now, has been unmanageable.

The leader – the product champion

What is the role of the design manager in the design circle? This person is a constant member of the design team. He will attend all the design meetings, lead the group and co-ordinate the design process. As such, he must be given authority. In fact, the design manager is the ideal person to be 'product champion', although in some companies the marketing manager will be just as suitable.

Obviously, the product champion is a most important role in the design team. The objective of a leader is to control and organize the activity of the design team, using the resources available in the best possible way. The leader should be encouraging the members of the team to perform optimally, while achieving the design team's objectives. He must help the members to understand their roles and their expected contribution. It will be necessary to encourage them to put their personal objectives in second place, where these conflict with the team's objectives, and to give positive feedback on their contribution and performance. Group leaders must be able to smooth over disagreements and unproductive competition between the team members, using tact, insight, detachment and firm control.

142

Design reviews

Cooper (1988), describing his 'gate' theory, says that: 'In order to weed out poor projects early in the process, there is a clear need for project evaluation points – where Go/Kill/Hold decisions are made on projects.' It is at design reviews where these decisions are taken. Cooper (1988) goes on to say: 'Gates serve a second purpose as well; they are the check points to ensure the quality of execution of process activities.'

We have found that those in the design circle should also provide the main input when holding design reviews. A design review is defined as a formal, documented, comprehensive and systematic examination of the capability of a design to meet the service design specification, to identify problems and propose solutions. They should be held whenever necessary and involve all who make a contribution. The purpose of the design review is to verify that the overall requirements of the market are being met by the proposed design, meeting performance, implementation and cost specifications. Design review meetings are vitally important, but very expensive in the cost of specialists' time. It is, therefore, essential that design reviews are well organized and managed to be effective decision-making forums, taking up as little time as possible.

Such is the importance given to design reviews that there is a committee writing an international (ISO) standard. (The British Standards Institute is also forming a committee to make proposals on the same subject.) In the first draft of the ISO standard it was advocated that design reviews should be held by a separate group not directly involved in the day-to-day organization of the design. But a totally separate group would not be fully conversant with all the aspects of the design under consideration. Furthermore, in a small organization, a suitable separate group may not be available. We believe that the best solution is a compromise: hold the design review with some members of the design circle who know why the decisions were made, supported by some people who understand the topics being discussed but are not actually in the day-to-day involvement of that particular design. This will add a more subjective/objective viewpoint to the decisions being made. The later drafts of the standard identify with this opinion by also proposing a 'mix' of some people who are directly involved in the design with some others from outside of the design group.

We also disagree with the – fortunately – declining view that it is only necessary to hold three design reviews, one before, one in the middle and one at the end of the project. This has even been said in books instructing people on how to design engineering products. This is far too few. The review at the beginning is really a preview, the one at the end is too late. This means that they are proposing only one effective design review in the entire design process.

Design reviews should be held whenever they are considered necessary (only you will know when that is), and at least after every stage of the design process or before a significant investment is to be made. The product champion ultimately decides when design reviews should be scheduled. Those involved should discuss progress to date and the continuation, or otherwise, of the design. Members must remember that the purpose of a design review is to make decisions that will smooth the progress of the service to being a success in the market. Therefore, individuals should make judgments only on evidence produced at meetings and not use it as an opportunity to 'win points' in the internal politics of the organization. Strong chairmanship can help to keep those at the meeting performing effectively.

In a typical design review the agenda should be circulated to all those who are to attend the meeting at least one week in advance. At the start of the meeting the design manager will give a formal introduction stating which documents each member should have received and the topics to be discussed. These topics will be presented by those responsible in a short verbal report which will be followed by a discussion. Questioning should be encouraged and at the end a decision taken. Ideally, the next point on the agenda should not be started until a decision is taken. This may be a call for action by some identified person and a date agreed for completion of this action. We have been to too many meetings where the only decision taken is to rediscuss the point at the next meeting. This should be avoided.

The minutes of each meeting must be recorded along with calls for action, decisions and recommendations. These minutes may be needed at some future date when a later version of the service is being designed or to provide legal back-up for use in design protection or product liability cases. Therefore, this documentation must be retained whilst the product is on sale or still in use.

The design review meetings should continue after the service goes on sale and throughout the sales life of that service. However good these review meetings are, they do not design anything and cannot be a substitute for good practice throughout other areas of the new product development process. If well planned, organized, controlled, documented and reported, it can increase confidence in the eventual success of the product.

Roles and responsibility matrix

With different people coming into the design circle at different stages in the design process, it can be quite difficult to control the roles and responsibilities of those involved. To help overcome this we have developed a matrix (*see* Fig. 9.4) which, from our consultancy, we have found assists with this control.

On the top horizontal axis the names and job titles of all those who will be involved in the design circle during the design of the service are noted. On the vertical axis the stages of the design process are written. This will result in a series of boxes, with a box for each person at each stage of the design. In the first place, only put a tick in the box to identify if a particular person

	Managing director	Product champion	Financial director	Marketing director	Sales personnel	Product engineering manager	Service manager	Agents	Purchasing manager	Continuous activity	Product-related activity	Number in design circle
Main management guidelines										✓		
Initial marketing input											✓	
Marketing desk research											✓	
Strategic specification										✓		
Relevant innovations										✓		
Competition analysis										✓		
Screening											✓	
Find product status											✓	
Service audit										✓		
Technical specification											✓	
Assemble full service specification											✓	

Fig. 9.4 Roles and responsibility matrix.

will be required to take part at any stage of the design process. The last vertical column is headed 'number in the design circle' and in this the total number of people involved at that stage of the design should be written. If this number exceeds nine then it would be advisable to split the design circle into two. Alternatively, it may be possible to divide this stage of the design process into two parts to be undertaken in series or, preferably, in parallel.

The other vertical columns, at the end of the matrix, indicate if the activity is product related, or continuous. For example, competition analysis and innovation seeking should continue all the time and one or two man-days each month should be devoted to this activity.

Having identified those in the design process, and where they make their contribution, the next stage is to give each their role and responsibility. Table 9.1 shows a list of possible responsibilities, which can be assigned to each member of the design circle. It is important that one person, but *only one* person, is identified to undertake the work. This avoids confusion with various people believing that others are doing the work when, in fact, nobody is. Several people may be expected to advise or be kept informed.

Table 9.1   List of responsibilities

Abbreviation	Responsibility
A	Executes the work
B	Must be consulted
C	Must be informed
D	Must advise/provide information
E	Must approve
F	Responsible for completion of the work

The matrix we have shown is an over-simplification. Usually at each stage there are several activities that must be completed. These should all be placed in the vertical column, with roles and responsibilities for all parts of these assigned.

This vertical column of activities can also be developed into a Gantt chart, with timescales placed on the horizontal axis, to aid with the scheduling of the design process.

=================================== **Summary** ===================================

- Design is a multidisciplinary team effort, where the design manager – 'product champion' – is the central, key person, controlling and organizing the design team's activities.

- Using design circles ensures that everybody who ought to be involved and make a contribution takes an active part and that that contribution is considered.

- The design circle has an organic structure, which enables people with different expertise and backgrounds to meet on an equal footing and communicate effectively with each other.

- A mechanistic structure may be used at the later stage of design when 'specialists' are involved.

- Design reviews must be well organized and managed meetings, held by the design circle and sometimes with help from others. These verify if objectives are being adequately met so that effective decisions can be made.

- It is possible to develop a roles and responsibility matrix. This will help with the control of those involved in the design circles at the different stages of the design process. Everyone will know who has been assigned to do what job and who had to be advised or kept informed on the various activities in the total design process.

Chapter 10

Training for Total Service Design

Introduction

Total Service Design is a new way of thinking and working for many organizations. It is the responsibility of all managers in the design team to ensure that all their staff and themselves are fully trained to be able to cross formal boundaries to contribute to the continued well-being of the organization now and in the future.

Unlike accountants or mathematicians who are employed to work in their specialized field, there are very few people around who have been trained to appreciate the all-embracing scope and multidisciplinary nature of the Total Design Process. As more people become aware of Total Design the situation may change and it may become possible to employ, for example, graduates with the appropriate skills required. But at present it is necessary to train the employees you need to design your new services.

The introduction of Total Service Design may call for major changes in the organization and as Stewart Miller (1990), the Director of Engineering of Rolls Royce plc says: 'Managing change successfully needs enlightened training.'

A significant point of Total Design is the formation of multidisciplinary teams. This means that employees will need training, for example, in leadership skills to be able to lead and direct these teams, and in team building and communications skills. Traditional skills may also have to be replaced as the organization needs people with new skills, such as software programmers if Computer Aided Design (CAD) is introduced into the design process. Design is about constant change and, therefore, must be associated with constant retraining. Training practices have to be organized and built into the design process.

Training is an essential element in the SDS. As Boddy and Buchanan (1986) stress: 'It not only affects people's abilities to operate equipment technically, but their overall confidence in, and willingness to use the system.' They go on to explain that introducing new technology means reviewing working practices, systems and skills. A 'general awareness' of the abilities of new technology is not enough.

One clear message for Britain in the next ten years is that there will continue to be a skill shortage and if your company uses skilled people you must either train them yourself or design them out of the system. In the manufacturing industry this has been going on for some years through automation. ('Will the last person out of the machine shop please switch the lights off.') This will spread to services in areas such as driving tube trains and any form of ticket collection and dispensing. Due to this automation people will become less visible in services this decade; products and systems will work but it will not be obvious how. Skills shortages will also spread to designers and they will become a scarce and valuable resource to be used wisely. This means good management of the Total Design process and a breaking down of existing barriers so that designers are devoting their time to designing products people actually want. This is down not only to efficient organization but also to effective education and training.

Customers in this country are used to having a choice in whatever they buy and have taught themselves to appreciate and buy good design. This choice will increase as an effect of the open market of 1992 when European trade barriers are removed. Competition will increase and, therefore, producers must train themselves to become more design conscious.

The training strategy

To be able to cope with and implement Total Service Design your organization needs a training strategy. This training must:

1. Identify the training needs for the management of Total Service Design.
2. Formulate the policy, establishing priorities and setting targets.
3. Implement the policy.
4. Keep records on the organization training performance.

In order that the members of the Total Design team are fully committed and motivated to perform at the highest level, training is an essential requisite.

Organizations that are concerned with the management of Total Service Design will want to consider how effective the existing methods and procedures are and whether these can be made more effective through a training policy. This policy should identify whether an organization is seeking qualified employees from the labour market or whether existing employees can be trained to meet the organization's changing skills – the latter requires a greater commitment to training.

The purpose of training is to achieve the appropriate level of performance from employees involved in the design team. This in turn follows the establishment of a business plan from which the manpower plans are developed.

149

If the organization employs a training manager this person must work together with senior managers in considering the organizational culture, the technology currently used, the reward system and, also, job descriptions and work design – how the work is actually done.

Therefore, a training strategy should include:

1. An overall assessment of the organizational needs regarding trained personnel when introducing Total Service Design.
2. An assessment of environment factors, including leadership style, in the organization.
3. An assessment of design team employees' needs and rewards.
4. A method for measuring results.
5. Flexibility to modify strategies where necessary.

The training process

Training at work is often classified into two categories:

1. Training – skills training.
2. Development – training at a managerial level.

It is not useful to use these two categories because both are types or styles of training, needing the same detailed, careful analysis and design in order to achieve objectives. The design and introduction of a training programme is the same as the design and introduction of a new service to the market. It should be considered as a total system and the principles of Total Service Design should be applied. Training is a structured process concerned either with acquiring abilities to perform successfully or with the maintenance of existing abilities.

This process involves well-defined phases of decision-making and action:

1. Identify the training needs and priorities:
   (a) To be able to deal with current weaknesses and to cater for future development – which jobs in the design team will planned training be needed for?
   (b) How many employees will need training for these jobs?
   (c) What are the priorities? Where are the most critical areas? Where will the training programme bring the quickest results or be the most immediately effective in the implementation of Total Design?
   (d) What resources and/or constraints will affect these decisions?

2. Examine the jobs chosen as a priority for training. Analyse the job and prepare:
   (a) A job description.
   (b) A job specification.

150

   (c)   Further analyse the skills, knowledge and attitudes required by members of the design teams in order to identify areas of difficulty which will thus affect the choice of what must be learned and of appropriate training techniques.

3.   Indicate, select and appraise the employees to be trained:
   (a)   What aptitudes and personal traits are required?
   (b)   Does the organization need to recruit and/or retrain present personnel?
   (c)   Which of the specified skills, knowledge and attitudes needed to be successful members of the design team do the identified employees already possess? This will show the knowledge shortfall or 'training gap', when compared to the job specification.

4.   Set the training objectives: What must the design team members be able to do and to what standard, after training? This is known as the 'criterion behaviour'.

5.   Analyse the training methods available and specify the steps to be taken in order to achieve the objectives.

6.   Plan the training programme, detailing the design of the specific training programme:
   (a)   In what sequence will the training take place?
   (b)   How will the training be done?
   (c)   Who will do the training (e.g. specialists skilled in the compiling of a service design specification or a professional experienced in leadership skills)?
   (d)   Where will the training take place (in-house or at a training/education establishment)?
   (e)   How long with the programme last?
   (f)   What resources are required? Are they available in the organization or can they be obtained.?

7.   Managing the training programme – the actual business of conducting the training programme that has been designed.

8.   Evaluate the impact of the training on the trainee and the organization:
   (a)   Has the training achieved its objectives?
   (b)   Has the right material been taught in the way and to the standard previously agreed?
   (c)   Has the trainee reached the expected level of proficiency?

9.   Check that the job has been done in a satisfactory manner. Following the training:
   (a)   Implementation – ensure that the trained personnel put into practice, in the workplace, the skills and knowledge acquired.

(b) Follow-up – this is an extension of the programme to reinforce learning. This may be in the form of further reading, instruction, discussion on what has been learnt.

Repetition of a skill that has been learnt is essential in order to reach a level of proficiency. This may automatically occur by being an active member of the design team or it may have to be organized. It should be part of the training process to assess the extent to which the new ideas, skills and motivation have an opportunity to be exercised and reinforced. Allow for recommendations to be made and steps to be taken to make good any lack of opportunity for the practice of what has been mastered. If the trainees are not able or not allowed to implement what they have learned, it may be necessary to identify further needs and return to step one in the training process. The completion of a training course should not be considered the end of the manager's obligation – training must be regarded as a continuous process. It is a cycle of activities as shown in Fig. 10.1.

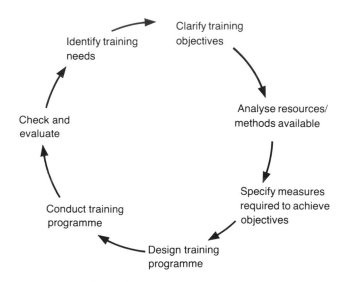

Fig. 10.1 The training cycle.

Summary

- The ability to establish a training programme and cycle and the development of a training strategy and policy is essential if you are implementing Total Service Design. Employees must be skilled in working within or leading multidisciplinary design teams to be able to meet the challenge of managing change in their organization.

- A training session or programme is likely to be an integral part of your service and, therefore, an important element on the SDS.

- The training programme itself is a service that has to be designed. To do this use the design process, in the same way as one would with any other service or product.

Aspects of service design

Chapter 11

Queuing – the sign of a bad service

Introduction

Over the past few years in industry, there has been a conscious effort to reduce stocks of raw materials, work in progress (WIP), buffer stocks and bottlenecks. Inventory is an expensive waste of space and ties up capital. Just-in-Time (JIT) is one philosophy where raw material and work in progress stocks are virtually eliminated; bottlenecks are shown up and must be removed if the system is to operate effectively. The aim of Just-in-Time was defined by Schonberger (1982) as a process to 'produce and deliver finished goods just in time to be sold, sub-assemblies just in time to be assembled into finished goods, fabricated parts just in time to go into sub-assemblies, and purchased parts just in time to be transformed into fabricated parts.'

The idea for JIT originally came from industrialists observing what happens in the retail sector. Engineers from Toyota, who were visiting America, were impressed by the way in which supermarket shelves were only stocked with a few items at any one time. These shelves were replenished whenever they became empty. From this basis has grown a whole series of continuous problem-solving practices, which force an organization to operate efficiently through the entire inventory chain.

In the context of a service, customers can often be compared to the raw material stock or the work in progress of a manufacturing plant. In this situation the stocks and bottlenecks are represented by people queuing. Stocks of components may be an inefficiency in the production context, but stocks don't complain. In a service excessive queuing or waiting will almost always result in customers forming a negative impression of the service and could lead to its eventual decline.

Another difference between a service and a manufactured product is that excess demand in a service cannot be stored to be dealt with later. If the service is not carried out when the customers require it then often this custom is lost to competitors. Queues cost money.

As recently as five years ago some 'experts' were still advocating their belief that a queue was a sign of an efficient service. If there was no queue then staff would be hanging around doing nothing. Shops that had customers queuing were considered efficient. It was thought that the number of staff should be reduced until there was evidence of people waiting. This meant the staff were always busy and working to their optimum (flat out). No one thought that the customer might not like queuing and, rather than wait, would seek the service elsewhere. As the customers went elsewhere the queues declined. The service again appeared 'inefficient' as there were not enough people waiting, but, through further staff reductions, the work 'efficiency' could be regained and the queues returned. This spiral could continue, presumably until most customers received the service elsewhere and the company either continued to operate in its reduced market niche or failed.

Fast-food outlets have made those running service operations realize, somewhat belatedly, that people not only do not like queuing, they will go as far as to select a service in which it can be avoided. In most queues those involved have little to do but just wait. As a result, time spent waiting is usually perceived as much longer than it really is. Next time you wait for a bus note the time that you started waiting and guess how long you have been waiting when the bus arrives. A check with your watch will make you realize that it was, probably, not as long as you originally thought, but you are still irritated.

Queuing and service design

There are two factors which must be considered when compiling your specification. If there are queues, can they be reduced or eliminated? If they can't be eliminated, how can the waiting be made more 'bearable'? The waiting may not even be visable. Tom Peters (1982) gives the example of the US delivery company, Federal Express, that never leaves the phone to remain unanswered for more than a couple of rings. This he perceives as being efficient, which it is in this one small aspect of the firm, but the impression it gives permeates through the whole company, so that customers believe the rest of the company must be efficient, whether it is or not.

There is little point in having the most up-to-date technology available if customers can't get into it. Make sure that potential customers can get to the contact that they require quickly and without fuss.

Once a service has a poor reputation it takes many years of providing a better than average performance to improve one's standing with the public. It is far easier to get and hold a good reputation by getting it right first time.

Customers will form an impression of an organization's efficiency as a result of their own experience. They do not think in terms of the fact that customer contact may only be a very small part of the whole service operation. Designing the interface with the customer is a critical part of the service design.

══════ **How to reduce or improve the queue** ══════

Initially identify the way in which people come into contact with the organization. Sometimes they take part in the total process, as in, say, shopping in a supermarket, or they may only make contact briefly such as phoning directory enquiries. Not all customers may go through the whole of the service on offer. If you can provide a 'standard' service, that is, one which is the same for everybody, it is easier to plan, process and automate. Unfortunately the 'personal' service that customers often require is at odds with service standardization. It may be possible, though, in some aspects, for example most hairdressers wash all customers' hair irrespective of what other treatment they may be having.

The optimum aim is the situation where one customer will appear at the stage in the process just as the previous one leaves it. This is a JIT approach.

Identify the route that most will take whilst using the service and ensure that it has been optimized. Plan the route through the service to minimize the distance travelled by customers and signpost this. This factor is important in the design of an airport, but may not be to your benefit if you wish to encourage the customers to partake in 'window shopping'.

Then consider if any waiting can be eliminated from the service. To eliminate queues you must first understand your service. This will involve measuring the demand pattern, which can be achieved as follows:

1. First define each process through which the customers pass – there may be more than one.
2. Breakdown the sequence into stages.
3. Then identify the demand pattern for the service through observation and time study.
4. Identify peaks and troughs which may occur in demand over the hour, day or year. This will make the demand pattern more predictable.
5. Identify where 'bottlenecks' occur during the process.
6. Eliminate, or improve, these bottlenecks through one or more of the methods that we will describe.
7. Implement the improvements and reappraise to ensure that the process runs more smoothly.

Quite often the elimination of a bottleneck will have the effect of moving the queue to another stage of the process further down the sequence. This will then be the focus of your next improvement.

Consider the operation of a restaurant as an example. Initially a customer may ring to reserve a table. The phone should be answered within five rings otherwise an answerphone should be available so that the customer can place the reservation. The answerphone message should state when any reservation can be confirmed. Very few restaurants operate a satisfactory 'out of hours' reservation system and this may be losing them significant custom.

When the customers arrive they should be greeted immediately and seated at their table or in a suitable waiting area. Customers find waiting to be more bearable when they feel that they are in 'the system' than waiting for it to start. Why not offer a free drink? A colleague said to us that people mind waiting less with a drink in their hand (note it's 'less' – they still mind waiting) and if the drink is free then they may consider it an advantage in being kept waiting. The cost of a drink is small in relation to the cost of the meal that they are about to purchase. Also it is perceived to be of greater value to the customer than the cost actually is to the restaurateur. For example, the worth of, say, a gin to the customer is about 80p, but in fact it is only 25p to the restaurateur.

Having an evening out in a restaurant is filled with waiting times and some of these pauses are more annoying than others – waiting for the menu, to have the order taken, for each course, for wine, coffee and the bill. Waiting for the bill is the most aggravating. Making a point of accepting the order for the wine and serving it promptly as well as having prepared starters can reduce waiting time. Design this into your service. Waiting for the main course to be served is often perceived as a good thing as it implies that the food is being freshly prepared and not just microwaved from frozen. The time of day is also important. At lunchtime the overall time allowed for a meal is often restricted by work. On the other hand, in the evening the meal is a social event and more time can be allocated to it.

Remember, much of the foregoing applies in other areas and with other processes.

There are basically two broad areas to consider if queues exist in your service: to overcome the peaks you should chase demand or adjust demand. The former is the better approach to take as it generally results in greater customer satisfaction.

Chasing demand

In this you endeavour to improve the service to cope with the large number of people passing through it. The most obvious way is by employing more people to attend to customers. This may be new personnel, who may be part-time or temporary staff, or perhaps a shift system or overtime could be operated. With some services there are front-of-shop and back-of-shop activities. The former activities tend to have a greater fluctuation in their demand patterns whereas the latter tend to be more stable. For example, in a post office there are the counter staff and those that work 'behind the scenes'. At periods of high demand, such as early on pension collection days, bring in those backroom personnel to work behind the counters until the peak has passed. This may involve retraining or multiskilling some of the staff.

If waiting must occur make it brief or pleasurable. Provide a suitably large area for people to wait. Put comfortable chairs in the waiting room and (recent) magazines. Why not offer free coffee which the customers can help themselves to? Music or a television in a waiting room can help pass the time and, in some cases, even earn money, an example being the pay televisions that have been in bus stations in America for the past 20 years.

New technology can assist in speeding the throughput of customers. Banks have been especially successful in this with the introduction of cashpoints. Supermarkets have speeded up queues with their recent investment in optical bar code readers (that also automatically adjust the information on stock levels), automatic cheque writers (where the details of the transaction is automatically filled in on the cheque and the customer just has to sign it) and EFTPOS UK (Electronic Funds Transfer at the Point of Sale) to clear payments made by electronic cashless shopping – the cardholder's current account is debited immediately and the retailer is instantly credited with the money. Automation may have the effect of taking the queue further down the system. In the case of supermarkets the bottleneck is now with people loading up their shopping. Such problems can be overcome by employing 'packers' to help customers with this loading. Match the technology or facilities to the available people. There is little purpose in having lines of well-equipped supermarket checkouts if there isn't the staff to man them.

Technology need not involve a large investment. It may only require a slightly faster method than is currently used, for example an egg and tomato slicer in a sandwich bar, or something that takes the load off busy periods like an answerphone.

It may be possible to improve the service to increase the numbers that can be accommodated merely by improving the efficiency of the staff involved. This requires training. Looking at the ergonomics of the service layout may also be a key to improving the throughput of customers.

Adjusting demand

For this you encourage customers to use the service at periods of low demand or restrict customers from using the service at times when demand is high. This will also help to avoid bottlenecks in the system. Identify periods when a service is less popular and under-utilized and make these times more attractive to all, or a section of potential customers. Differential pricing, e.g. 'happy hour' in a wine bar, low-price 'pensioner days' for certain services or out of season low-cost holidays can smooth demand. Other examples are the 'cheap rate' telephone charges and London Transport Capital Cards for lower cost travel at off-peak times. In some places it is worthwhile closing at unpopular times. Many shops are closed on Mondays.

At quiet times in the service, entertainment could be provided such as a band or special food or fancy dress nights. Ideas such as these can overcome the problem of, once having made the service efficient, how this efficiency in operation can be utilized throughout the week.

As we all have been 'fed up' with waiting at one time or another in our lives, why not consider this aspect of customer contact in your service design specification? There is also an opportunity to be innovative in your attempts to make queuing more bearable.

One much quoted case was that of a lift in an office block that operated slowly and often had people waiting for it. Engineers were called in to see if the lift could be made to operate faster or an additional lift could be fitted but both of these options proved to be impossible. The 'solution' was a series of full length mirrors that were placed outside the lift on each floor, people could then amuse themselves looking at themselves, or others, whilst waiting (Rivett and Ackoff 1963).

Another example can be seen at Disneyland. Waiting in line is a fact of life for most rides at the height of the season, but this is made more acceptable by having some form of 'visual experience' around every corner of the queue. Disneyland could even expand and improve on this feature. They could make queues with more corners in them so that the view is constantly changing. They could also entertain the queue with jugglers or 'street theatre'. The queue outside the waxwork museum at Madam Tussaud in London has used this form of street entertainment to good effect.

These companies have planned and acted correctly. First they tried to eliminate the problem, and when no solution could be found, they made the waiting more acceptable or even enjoyable. This philosophy should be followed with any service.

Appointment systems

The simplest way to avoid queues is to have an appointment system, but it must be one that works. Turning up at the appointed time only to be kept waiting is one of the most annoying aspects of queuing. One London hospital makes the times for all appointments at one particular clinic for 1 p.m. None of the doctors are scheduled to arrive until 2 p.m. and therefore the minimum wait is one hour – most have to wait a good deal longer. 'Old hands' turn up around 4 p.m. often to be seen within half an hour. An effective appointment system takes some management skill to organize but apart from leading to greater customer satisfaction it can also release valuable space set aside for waiting. This could then be used for more profitable purposes such as a clinic room or an extra service bay. Consider private hospital services – a lot of their apparent advantage is stated to be down to a reduction in waiting, be it in waiting to see a doctor or waiting some months for an operation. People are prepared to pay a great deal of money to 'jump' these queues, such is the importance of this aspect of service design.

Some of the best 'appointment systems' have been organized by airline companies who want to maximize the usage of their planes. An aeroplane lying idle on a runway is wasting thousands of pounds per hour in landing fees, depreciation and lost opportunity costs. This idle time is minimized through queuing theory. Similar theories are applicable to many other service operations such as clinics, car servicing, car valeting, post offices or hairdressers, etc. The principle is simple. Identify the broad categories of service and how often they occur. In the case of planes, it may be that a jumbo jet takes 1½ hours to unload, clean, undertake minor servicing and reload. This may take only 45 minutes for other planes. Assuming that one-third of all planes are jumbos and that they arrive in a random fashion (which is less likely in the case of planes than it is with customers having a particular requirement), the appointment system can be calculated with a dice. Table 11.1 shows the system being calculated.

Table 11.1 'Dice throw' appointments system

Allocate numbers 2 and 5 to jumbo jets and 1, 3, 4 and 6 to other planes.

Dice number thrown	Service time	Time of appointment
2	1½	00 – 1.30
4	¾	1.30 – 2.15
3	¾	2.15 – 3.00
5	1½	3.00 – 4.30
5	1½	4.30 – 6.00

Over a period of such simulations the system shows the type of appointment system that can be operated and generally it has been found to work well. Only when some unpredictable occurrence takes place does the system break down, such as a technical failure that puts the plane out of action causing delays at airports. Many of these can be avoided through planned maintenance.

In many cases, such as in a dentist's surgery, it is possible for the receptionist to ask the patient a few simple questions to find out if the visit will take five minutes or half an hour, or on subsequent visits for a particular treatment see from the dentist's notes, and the 'random' nature of the appointment system can be removed. Furthermore, with experience, it is possible to 'fine tune' the system so that waiting of no more than a few minutes can be ensured in all but the most unexpected situation. The appointment system can, therefore, be organized as in Table 11.2. The process seems 'haphazard' but, in practice, it works quite well and can avoid a full dentist waiting room. 'Tea breaks' etc. can also be scheduled into the systems.

Table 11.2 Dentist's appointments system

		Dice number
Preliminary check-up	10 mins (all patients)	
Cleaning	15 mins (approximately 50% of patients)	1,2,3,5
Minor surgery	30 mins (approximately 30% of patients)	3, 4
Major surgery	60 mins (approximately 15% of patients)	2

Dice number thrown	Time in	Check-up time and treatment (open 12.00 noon)	Time over
1	12.00	10 + 15	12.25
3	12.25	10 + 30	1.05
4	1.05	10 + 30	1.45
1	1.45	10 + 15	2.10
6	2.10	10 + 0	2.20
2	2.20	10 + 60 + 15	3.45
6	3.45	10 + 0	3.55

The work involved in designing an appointment system is small and the cost can be extremely low, yet it reaps rewards in improving customer satisfaction and efficiency of the service. The key is to identify what the main groups of service product on offer are, how long this aspect of the process usually takes and how frequently this occurs. To any manager who really understands his business these are not difficult to ascertain.

Many services operate, by necessity, without an appointment system. It would be foolish to expect to have to make an appointment to buy a stamp or pay for your newspaper delivery. It is still possible, however, to arrange the services on offer to ensure a fast throughput of customers and to avoid bottlenecks. Customers don't like cluttering up space on your premises any more than you enjoy the congestion, noise and complaints that this inefficiency brings about. Therefore plan to avoid queues as part of your service design.

Consider the following improvement to a commonly experienced queue. You arrive at an airport to have your passport collected whilst leaving the aircraft. You are led into a lounge where you can be served coffee. When all the formalities are complete you are then taken into the customs hall where your cases await you. No queues and all very civilized – an impossible dream? This is the normal procedure at Tirana airport in Albania. Admittedly the planes and people are few but we propose that a similar system could be incorporated at some other small airports in which the throughput of passengers is fairly small. Why not arrange for passengers to sit in the comfort of a lounge whilst their luggage is being unloaded from the plane?

If queues are inevitable they can be designed to move quickly. The Post Office and banks have already made some progress with this. They initially copied the American system of having several windows served by a feeder queue. In itself, this doesn't reduce waiting time but makes it fairer as the effect of any one 'slow' customer will not hold up the entire queue, and it also overcomes the individual annoyance of being stuck in one queue when the other queues around you seem to move more quickly. They then separated out service points for particularly fast (and to a lesser extent, slow) services and these customers can be quickly serviced. Examples are the 'stamps only' service point in a post office or the 'less than six items' checkout in a supermarket. Perhaps a 'price and delivery' window in a car service centre would alleviate much of the waiting when information only is required.

There has even been research to ascertain whether people prefer to be in a short slow-moving queue or a long fast-moving one – the results seem to be inconclusive.

Recently we decided to buy a new car. Rather than go to the sales showroom we decided to ascertain how good their service was. We went to the spares department built on the side of the showroom of this large French car company and endeavoured to find out the price, delivery and cost of fitting a particular spare part. The car showroom was filled with the usual display of cars and we counted eight sales persons. There were, at that time, no customers. On the other hand there were several customers in the spares department being served by one, clearly undertrained, operative. We timed our wait at half an hour and during this wait we learned from a couple of garage mechanics that:

1. They always have to wait a long time at this place to be served.
2. Often the parts they require are not available.
3. The parts were excessively overpriced in their opinion.
4. The staff did not seem to know much about their product.
5. They were apparently poorly managed: 'There never seems to be anybody in charge around here.'
6. The time spent by the mechanics collecting parts meant that they always had to give their customers a high quote for jobs on these French cars because they had to cost in the inefficiency of this operation.

The half hour convinced us that this make of car was not the one we should own.

Now supposing this department had been efficiently organized to virtually eliminate waiting. Initially we would have determined the price, delivery and fitting cost quickly – we never did find out the last of these. We would not have met complaining customers because these would also have been served quickly. The fact that nobody appeared to be in charge would still not be apparent, but this would not have mattered as the customers would see a smoothly running service and assumed good management. Work done on these cars would be less expensive – half an hour at typical garage prices is £12 on the bill.

What was the solution? Training and organization. The single server would have operated faster had he been properly trained. Retraining of some of the showroom sales staff could enable them to stand in at busy times in the spares department when the showroom was quiet, as in our visit. A side counter could be arranged for customer enquiries on price, availability, and for 'quick' purchases such as replacement bulbs, wiper blades, car valeting equipment, etc.

Such a service should be computerized to show instantly what is in stock and this system should also identify stock levels and place reorders if these are getting low – MRP (Materials Requirement Planning). We found all this available in the service department of a British car company – there was room for improvement but it was considerably better than our previous experience.

An example of a service, which has improved in the 1980s has been car exhaust fitting centres 'while you wait'. A blown exhaust no longer means that the car is off the road for half a week and a hefty bill, plus the problem of journeying to and from the garage without the car.

The key to improving a service is to:

1. Identify the problem.
2. Measure the problem (e.g. by observation or time study).
3. Consider alternative solutions.
4. Select the optimum solution.
5. Implement the solution.
6. Check the result is an efficient solution and modify it if necessary.

Remember to identify the variation in the service. Demand may vary by the hour as in a transport system. Demand may vary by the day as in a hairdressers. Demand may vary by the season as with car sales or by the weather as in ice-cream sales. Demand may even vary by the year if the service is related to a particular event such as the Olympic Games. Until the demand pattern is understood it is very difficult to optimize the service to avoid queues and to maximize customer satisfaction.

All this is part of service design. The design manager is responsible for ensuring that the way in which people pass through the service has been fully considered and the service designed for the benefit of the customer.

Summary

- People queuing is often a sign of a badly designed service. As part of total design the manner in which people take part in, or interface with, the service is an important consideration. Queues must preferably be avoided or eliminated. Sometimes this is not possible and in such cases waiting must be made more comfortable or more acceptable to the customer.

- If queues exist in a service where the demand pattern varies consider methods to chase demand, that is to increase the volume that can be handled at peak periods.

Alternatively, adjust demand, which means smoothing the demand pattern so that the existing process operates more efficiently for greater periods of the day. A combination of both tactics may be necessary.

Chapter 12

Technology transfer

Introduction

From 1780 to 1880 Britain was the world's leading exporting nation. In 1946 Britain still had 25 per cent of world trade, by the mid-1970s this was down to 8 per cent and now we have about 6½ per cent. In 1983 we went into deficit for the first time in 200 years in our balance of payments for manufactured goods. This aspect of the deficit has continued to grow and currently stands at about £12 billion.

But how does this affect services? Only about 11 per cent of services are exportable compared with over 90 per cent of manufactured goods. On the other hand, many services 'ride on the back' of manufactured products and this means that, increasingly, services operate with, or through, products made abroad. A car showroom may display foreign cars, computer programmers may be writing programs on foreign computers. Even more we are becoming 'a nation of shopkeepers' (Napoleon) manufacturing less ourselves and selling each other products that are made abroad.

In this chapter we will be discussing the dangers that the service sector is likely to experience from an invasion of competition from overseas. In many respects, the situation that will occur in the service sector in the near future mirrors that which happened in the manufacturing sector. But there is still time for service organizations to avoid this decline – one way is through Total Design. Through the implementation of Total Design of services, organizations will be better prepared to take on the competition that will threaten home markets from organizations based overseas. Well-designed services that meet the customer needs and incorporate the most up-to-date technology will be the only way to ensure a continued existence in today's fiercely competitive world in the service sector. Total Design will equip your organization with the products to take on the best in the world and win.

What happened in manufacturing

The British government in the past decade has put great store in the belief that the decline in the manufacturing sector can be made up by an expansion in the service sector. This is true, up to a point, but it has also been estimated that we would have to have 54 per cent of the total world market for services to be able to replace our manufacturing base completely and avoid a balance of payments deficit. Also evident has been the expansion in services which has resulted in an increase in white-collar workers and a decline in blue-collar workers. This is a world-wide phenomenon but it is happening faster in the USA and the UK than in most other parts of the industrialized world. On the negative side the non-exportable nature of most services has meant that the efforts to promote and expand this sector have resulted in the balance of payments problem that will remain for some years. People want products and these products are a measure of their status and standard of living. Although these products may be sold and serviced in this country, more than ever they will have their origins abroad.

In the long term there will be little effect in most service organizations. It will not matter to those employed in a service company if they are fixing a TV made in Britain or Japan, or cleaning clothes made in Britain or Italy. There may, perhaps, be problems in the availability and cost of spare parts but, that apart, they could operate in much the same manner. But if 11 per cent of services can be exported about the same percentage can be imported and it is worth considering if, therefore, some sectors of British service design are under threat.

To clarify the picture it is worthwhile looking at what happened in the manufacturing sector. In the 1950s it was discovered that the most successful *innovative* companies in America were generally not, as one would expect, the most highly automated, but the most labour intensive. This is the sort of result that one would have expected from an underdeveloped country. It could be explained by the fact that being a new product, such as an aircraft, this product was assembled by people who were highly educated or skilled. The automation was incorporated at a later stage when the design was less innovative and had reached a point where it had 'settled down'. This is when the manufacturing process became more stable and, therefore, more predictable, making it worthwhile investing in process equipment.

Around the same time the 'technology lag' was identified. This lag was the number of years that a country would take before it could catch up on the innovators – who were, at that time, usually American. The average technology or imitation lag in the 1950s was typically two to five years for America and West Germany, five years for the UK and France. With some underdeveloped countries, though, it could take 10 – 40 years to catch up on this new technology. This time period was reduced in the 1960s and certain countries 'leapfrogged' in their grasp of technology, missing out some of the in-between stages. An example of this is the Chinese telephone system. An electronic system has been adopted and the Chinese have missed out the now outdated electromechanical stage of technology.

Even allowing for this, certain countries were able to catch up faster and the most obvious of these was Japan. Eventually they were able to incorporate many electronic developments only two years from their appearance in the American market. Furthermore, these Japanese copies were often better engineered and subsequently more successful on the market than the American equivalent. This has become a serious problem with many US companies as they can no longer claw back the cost of research and development with new product sales before the market has been taken over by a Japanese competitor. As a result the American semiconductor industry is falling further behind that of Japan.

Professor Chris Freeman (1988), a fascinating talker and writer from the Science Policy Research Unit (SPRU) at Sussex University, has investigated how the Japanese are able to manage their new product development processes to be apparently so efficient and has identified the following four reasons.

1.   The Japanese developed a new method of producing new products. Their industry integrated design with production which gave them shorter lead times and better control of quality. They did this through a more lateral (organic) flow of information and communication. Industry in America was still organized on the less efficient hierarchical (mechanistic) structure.

The effect of this integration of product and process design was to reduce lead times in car design in Japan to 60 per cent of the time taken in America.

2.   Improving education and training in Japan ensures a good supply of skilled people. More students in Japan stay on at school until they are eighteen than is the case in Europe or America. Of these, a higher percentage go on to further education and of these many more do engineering. Japan has twice the number of graduates than America and the ratio is even greater in electronics. Compared with Britain the figure is much greater. Japan has ten times the number of qualified engineers than Britain. Although the average British engineer in fact produces more exports than his Japanese counterpart, it's just that there are so few British engineers endeavouring to produce these exports.

Following their formal education at university Japanese students receive an intensive industrial training during which they learn to take part in these organic systems. This is not unlike the now defunct British postgraduate apprenticeship system. The newcomers into Japanese industry are also given responsibility and allowed to make decisions.

The system isn't perfect. Professor Sasha Kennaway (1989) of Imperial College, London University, who has the unusual combination for someone from Britain of being able to speak Japanese as well as knowing a vast amount about product design, has travelled in Japan and visited both industry and universities. He found that teaching in the Japanese universities is rigid, consisting of uninterrupted lectures given to very large classes. There is little contact between those who teach in these universities and those who work in industry. Both the students and teachers in universities were poorly motivated. Japanese industry has found that they have to give graduates a thorough training to make up for the deficiencies of their formal education system. Japanese companies are often happier to employ what Sasha Kennaway calls 'mavericks', who are students that may have failed some of their formal exams, but are more innovative and less rigid in their thinking.

3. Big investment in new products requires money borrowed for long periods. In Japan, bank conglomerates use short-term investment to fund long-term finance. This enables companies to borrow money to invest in long-term projects without the need to appease the short-term investor, who is typical of those who invest on the Stock Exchange. The typical British or American investor is unlikely to be interested in supporting any project in which there will be no return for twenty years. A profit in six months is the usual requirement, which is one reason why British and American companies only have short-term aims, which prevent research into the new technologies that will be paramount in the early part of the next century. To undertake long-term research that will provide the major innovations of the next century, it is necessary to have investment for a long period of time. This 'patient money' is necessary if we are to compete on a world stage with advanced products in the future.

One example is research into biotechnology. In Japan this work is being led by steel companies where it is accepted that there will be no return for twenty years. These companies will even have to train the people before they will be able to undertake this research.

These companies are protected when in this vulnerable position by an arrangement of cross holdings which makes them impossible to be taken over.

4. This technological innovation is only possible through the orchestration of the Ministry of International Trade and Industry (MITI). This organization was set up in the mid-1950s to allocate scarce resources of raw materials to those companies who could use them best to generate exports. They then identified certain product areas where they sought a world market. These were not to be labour intensive products but those with a large world market and high added value – cameras, motor cycles, cars, for example. The rest is history. In Japan 30 per cent of the GNP is reinvested every year to ensure that they retain their lead in the future. They are not hindered by significant military expenditure that often causes an emphasis on technology that only has a limited world market.

Of interest, and perhaps a warning to the West, is that those features which have been shown to benefit Japan in winning technology markets have been shown by Freeman to be even more apparent in Korea. In Korea, and to some extent Taiwan also, the Japanese model has been copied but with an even greater emphasis on education. Korea is training an even higher ratio of engineers than Japan. They also have the added advantage of a low wage economy that will make their products even more attractive on the world market.

The threat to services

Now consider the threat of lost markets due to competition from the Far East in relation to those services that can be imported. It is now apparent to the Japanese that what they have done to win Western markets for manufactured goods is equally applicable for some services. The Japanese have pursued the development of the infrastructure and methods of diffusion that served them so well with manufactured products but now for services. They have earmarked banking as one area ideally suited for this approach. Their first attempts to break into this area resulted in them 'getting their fingers burned', but such is their endeavour, they have been continuing in their efforts in the face of losses that would have frightened off many Western companies. Frances Moss, a senior lecturer in accounting and finance at the Polytechnic of Central London, in her article in *The Independent* (1989), identified these losses as 'at least $10 million apiece that the big four securities houses, Nomura, Yamaichi, Daiwa, and Nikko, made in the US in 1988'.

The hotel industry, apparently, is another example where the combination of communications coupled with a use of technology and available finance can be used to develop, the Japanese believe, world-beating new services. Currently, British-owned hotels have the largest share of the world market. As yet, though, the Japanese are backward in their development of retailing.

The threat in many service areas is very real and will not disappear. A defence against this competition, through the design of better services, seems to be one of the few ways to ensure a continued existence.

What has been described as the Japanese recipe for success in many ways is Total Design. What they have identified is a need to break down the barriers between those in organizations so that communication becomes more effective. Design in most Japanese companies is organic. They now also know when it is best to innovate or imitate and for some time they have known that quality and reliability are paramount in their design of their consumer products.

But, in the stages in which design goes through, the Japanese have one great weakness – market research carried out at the start of the design process. Japanese companies don't manage the entire design process; they 'rarely spend time doing detailed market research studies . . . far better, they argue, to rush even half baked ideas into the shops' (Valery 1989). This can lead to customer dissatisfaction.

Having spoken to people from Japanese companies, large and successful companies with growing world markets, we have found that they know of this weakness. They are efficient at producing world-beating products through the methods described, but as they have so many engineers and technicians they are able to design a large number of products that can be tried first on their home markets.

Design in Japan is very much a numbers game. Visitors to Japan are often impressed by the wide range of products that are available there that they never see elsewhere. Shops in Tokyo are filled with many new products that never reach the wider markets of the West. As an example, recently we were shown an electronic letter opener that had been manufactured by a very well known Japanese electronics company. It was novel but clearly less efficient than any traditional method of opening letters and, in fact, it managed to cut a letter in half when we tried it.

The point we are making is that many products are designed in Japan. They put them on the shelves in their shops and if these products are unsuccessful they will remove them from the market and replace them with other new products. Because of the large number of engineers and designers that they have trained, the Japanese companies are able to do this far more than we can in Britain. When the Japanese do identify something that has potential they then proceed to undertake market research more seriously, 'fine tuning' the product for individual markets. For example, cars they export to Italy have louder exhausts as Italians like a 'sporty' sound to their cars and cars for export to Germany have softer suspensions than those exported elsewhere in Europe.

They have the design process well organized once they have decided what needs designing, but, very often, they decide on the wrong product. They have not yet organized the link between the market and design correctly and, therefore, they do not always provide the products that the customer wants. Knowing this weakness you can be sure that they are working on it and probably using research that has emanated in the West to overcome this problem.

In the service sector they cannot play this numbers game as their superiority in skilled manpower is not so pronounced. But they still have advantages in other areas – finance, technology and organization – and these advantages that made their products world-beaters and are now being applied in services. By following the Total Design practice it should be possible to compete with almost anybody on equal footing and, providing that the necessary skills and finance are made available, to identify potential markets and design the service to win them.

There is another dimension to this. Some services rely on visitors from abroad for their survival – the tourist industry is an obvious example – but how would some shops in Oxford Street survive without the custom of people from overseas? Several private hospitals depend for their survival on a steady influx of wealthy patients who cannot get an equivalent quality of service in their own country. Would these companies survive if an equivalent service was made available to them in their own countries? In fact, there has already been serious cutbacks in the UK private medical sector as a result of the provision of first-class hospitals in the Gulf.

If our shops are mainly selling products made abroad the tourist can probably already get these at home, leaving only smoked salmon, tartan scarves and a few other British made rarities on their shopping list.

If your service relies on visitors from abroad it could be under threat from being provided abroad. Perhaps it should be provided abroad by you?

Summary

- In the manufacturing sector in the UK and USA there has been a radical decline. Although much of the resulting unemployment has been taken up by the service sector many of these services rely on imported manufactured products. The result is a balance of payments problem.

- The factors that made Japan so successful in manufacturing are now being applied to some service sectors. This could result in a decline in our involvement in these sectors and a loss of these markets.

- In the service sector there is still time to plan to avoid the decline that happened to our manufacturing industry. One way is through Total Design.

A worked example of total service design

Chapter 13

'Come Clean'

Introduction

In this chapter we show how the service design process works in a fictional company, an upholstery and carpet cleaning business called 'Come Clean'.

In the introductory chapter of this book we stated that the procedures for designing a new product are very like those for starting a new business. So, in this worked example of the system we have taken the case of two women who are investigating the prospect of starting a small business operating from a room in one of their homes. The business is to be financed by their redundancy pay from their previous jobs and this totals £5,000, plus a borrowing facility of a further £3,000, if required.

The example is purely artificial but the stages that the two women take, the layered approach and the completion of each layer before starting the next, mirrors the proposals made in the design process described in Chapter 8. The decisions taken are known to be typical of a much wider range of service product design and serve only to show the process in practice. In a larger company the procedures would certainly be more formal and should be presented in the form of reports and memoranda.

2 April 1991: Come Clean

Amy paused from eating her working lunch. 'There are three pizza places in the High Road and this company makes the worst.'

'Yes, but they are the only one that delivers,' answered Carol, 'and we don't want to waste valuable time going to the take-away when we should be discussing my new business proposal. Have you noticed recently how successful new products, if not advertised as luxury goods or labour saving, have been aimed at saving people time?'

'Or altering the time frame to suit the customer, such as late-night shopping, video-taping television programmes to view at a more convenient time, even pub opening hours, I suppose,' continued Amy, pushing the last quarter of her pizza to one side. 'OK, so what's this "business proposal"?'

'My idea is for an upholstery and carpet cleaning business,' Carol announced. 'Let me put you in the picture. Friends of mine know a couple who used to run a carpet and upholstery cleaning service on the other side of town. Well, they were a married couple, but have now split and the ex-wife has moved back home to the North. The man, Alan Hallam, has all the equipment, including four machines, which he wants to sell off at a knock-down price of £800. The machines usually sell at £400 each. He will hold on to them until the beginning of July. He has already run a similar operation in this area and says that he was overwhelmed with work and that two people were enough to provide a good customer service. (Reacting to market pull and an effective sales unit). What do you reckon, shall we use our redundancy pay to buy the equipment and go into business, operating from my spare room?'

'Slow down Carol, the idea sounds great and, in principle, I'm in full agreement, but let's go about this in a sensible manner. I don't want to blow all my redundancy pay on a half-baked idea. After all, I could use the money for a holiday or leave it in the building society to gain interest. You sort out all the details about starting a business, government grants, insurance rates, etc. [Outside the sphere of this book.] We want to keep a tight control on the likely costs of this venture. I'll look at this particular service design using this design process. I'll be the "product champion", and initially it will be a two-person design circle.'

'That's fine by me Amy. You are right, let's take our time and do this properly. Anyway, I've thought of a name for the company – "Come Clean". With our combined redundancy pay we have £5,000, so let's limit the expenditure to that £5,000 for the service design side and not borrow yet. We'll keep a tight control on that,' agreed Carol. 'You press on with the "strategic specification" and we'll meet for a discussion next week. A week should be long enough to make some serious inroads. You had better put your findings in a formal report, if we are going to be business-like. First, I'll start with the "main management guidelines" and the "initial market input".'

Layer 1

9 April 1991: Main management guidelines (Carol)

1. No restrictions on distribution methods.
2. The work will be undertaken by Amy and Carol. No subcontract at this stage.
3. To provide between 35 and 50 hours work each per week for two people.
4. Provide a profit of £18,000 in the first year (a salary for each).
5. No specified turnover as long as the other criteria are met.

6.   No initial borrowing, but to recoup the initial outlay of up to £5,000 plus 20 per cent to cover the interest we would have made if we had left the money in the bank for a couple of years (lost opportunity costs).

7.   Be organized within a maximum of 55 hours per person each week management time, working five days a week.

8.   The only technology to be used will be that which Amy and Carol are already familiar with, or can be learned within two days.

9.   Both Carol and Amy will be paid the same after expenses have been deducted.

10. It must be known that the service will, or will not, be marketable by 1 July 1991 (so that Alan Hallam can be informed).

11. Operate from a room in Carol's house.

(There is management commitment to the idea and financial control.)

'You can see that I added two extra guidelines. Others were not relevant in this case. There will be an emphasis in the business on quality and reliability and at this stage we have the capabilities to be successful,' added Carol.

═══════════ Layer 2 ═══════════

24 April 1991: Initial market input (Carol)

I have outlined an initial marketing specification from what we have been discussing and also from various books and papers in the library. I've also asked twenty-five people, who own their own home and live in our likely range of operations, a questionnaire so that we can fill in the gaps in the initial marketing specification. Furthermore, I then analysed the results and asked the respondents the feedback questionnaire. The results were as follows:

1.   Come Clean will be used exclusively by home owners, of which there are plenty in our anticipated area of operations.

2.   We can reach customers by visiting them with all the necessary equipment in a 15 cwt van.

3.   Quite frankly there are far more potential customers than we could hope to reach and, as Alan Hallam says, there appears to be a demand larger than we could hope to meet in a year. Probably about 5,000 potential customers for us and our competitors. How many of these we can expect depends on our prices and quality of service. We need about 650 customers per year or 13 per cent of the available work.

4.   Initially we reckon on between £30 and £45 per half day clean at a rough guess. [*Note:* In practice there would be a scale of charges depending on the size and how many carpets are to be cleaned. The one price is given here to keep the example more simple.]

179

5.   Those who tend to have their carpets cleaned generally continue to do so every three years. Of course this varies, but this is a good average. If the job is well done there are usually repeat orders.

6.   The market still appears to be growing and it is not just a 'fad' type of service.

7.   Customers generally seek carpet and upholstery cleaners through advertisements in the local papers or through *Yellow Pages*. Quite a few customers are attracted to the service from handbills pushed through their letter-boxes or by notices in newsagents windows. Word of mouth from other satisfied customers is another important way that customers get to hear of a company.

8.   Customers generally telephone to make an appointment. They expect a visit within two weeks of a call.

9.   The woman of the house still seems to be responsible for keeping the house clean and tidy. We can expect most calls from housewives for midweek cleaning and working women for the service at the weekend (usually Saturday). This means that we ought to operate between Tuesday and Saturday.

10.   'Spring cleaning' is still a fact of life. The highest demand will be in March, April and May and there is also a peak in demand during September and October. On either side of Christmas there is another peak in demand, as people clean their houses before visitors and then have to clean up again after them. This will determine when we can take our holidays and when we can arrange maintenance and do the administration.

11.   There are some competitors, I have found three that are likely to operate in our area. These are Apex Service Cleaners, Uniclean and New Pin Cleaners. All seem quite proficient. I will be looking more into these in the next layer of the process, if we still think the idea has potential then.

12.   Quality and reliability are the most important areas on which to compete. Customers have a fear that their furniture and carpets will be shrunk, stained or the colours will run. The other area on which to compete is to arrive when we say that we will. Several potential customers have said that they have taken days off work and then the cleaners let them down by not appearing. The usual effect of this is that the customer will cancel the order and calls in another company.

13.   I think we can offer a more personal and friendly service than the competition. Also, perhaps add inside paintwork cleaning (see below).

The results of the 'feedback questionnaire' were quite successful. I gave our sample of people a report covering the points that I had originally asked of them. It was quick and easy to fill in and 20 gave it back to me when I called.

1. All thought my report an accurate description of what they said.

2. All thought my report an accurate description of their cleaning requirements.

3. All stated that our list of their service requirements was accurate, thus confirming the accuracy of the report.

4. Ten indicated that the report was helpful in giving an understanding of the type of service they needed. Ten confirmed that they are not interested in what we are proposing.

5. Not surprisingly, in this case, they couldn't suggest any improvements in the way we have done this market research.

6. Of those who were interested eight of the ten thought we had got it just about right. The proposed service, at this stage, would appear to be suitable for their requirements.

7. Three people said that they would also like the additional feature of having inside paintwork cleaned to be incorporated into our service. Perhaps we could think about this improvement later?

8. None said that the paint cleaning was essential to their requirements. They thought between £5 – £10 per room would be a fair price for this additional feature.

30 April 1991: Report by Amy

I have completed some more work on how the service can be operated and what we can charge. If we do 16 service cleans per week, operating between Tuesday and Saturday and doing administration on Friday, assuming that we can only get work for 80 per cent of the time that we are available, that is 563 cleans per year (44 weeks' work and 8 weeks' holiday). If we pay ourselves £9,000 for the first year, I have estimated the cost of depreciation, fuel and van running expenses, etc., at £3,000 in the first year. We also need to include an amount for promotion, insurance for ourselves and the equipment:

	£
Wages and National Insurance etc.	21,000
Cleaning machines	800
Van and running costs etc.	3,000
Promotion	200
	£25,000

Cost of cleans £25,000
                 563

That is over £44 per clean, which, I think, is more expensive than the competition if we add VAT (£50.60). I don't think this idea is going to work. We had better meet to discuss the situation.

3 May 1991: Meeting

'I think most of your report is basically right, Amy, but you are under-utilizing our capability. It should only take half a day to do the administration and only one of us need to do it (we could take it in turns). Also, we could do a lot of this administration at those times when business is slack. That means we can probably do up to 20 calls per week, Tuesday to Saturday, which is 704 service calls per year which, on your figures, works out at about £35.50 per clean plus VAT and this gives us an adequate initial wage.

'You are also forgetting our unused machines. We could rent these on a DIY basis, either on collect and return, or deliver – that is an untapped market – like the pizzas we had delivered.

'Travelling in London may be a problem though. If we are operating on a five-mile radius, it could be ten miles between the two service points.

'Consider four customers, A, B, C and D, at the limit of our operating radius and the maximum possible distance from each other.

Visit to first customer and drop off machine and first operative.	Base	to A	5 miles
Then across to the next customer. Second operative park and do clean.	A	to B	10 miles
Second operative returns to pick up the first operative at lunch time.	B	to A	10 miles
Then on to the first afternoon customer. Drop off machine and first operative.	A	to C	10 miles
And then the second afternoon customer. Second operative. Park and do clean.	C	to D	10 miles
Second operative returns to the first afternoon customer to pick up first operative.	D	to C	10 miles
Then home.	C	to Base	5 miles
		TOTAL	60 miles

In this case that could be 60 miles of town driving in one day.

'It wouldn't in actual fact as D and B, and A and C, would be pretty close so we would swop the order round and do A and C in the morning and B and D in the afternoon but even so we could be driving, probably, 30 miles in town a day.

'Just taking the service calls we can do it for £41 per visit with VAT included, which is very competitive, but I think we ought to charge quite a bit more than the cheapest, after all would you risk getting your carpet cleaned by the cheapest? This implies poor quality even if this isn't so. Let's provisionally set our price at £46 inc. VAT. This will give us a good enough return to invest in more, or better, equipment in the future (over £3,000 per year). the DIY business only adds to this. I think it looks viable.

'I suspect that carpet cleaning will be fairly seasonal. During the quiet periods we can have the van and equipment serviced. The turnover means we will have to be registered for VAT. We can see how that goes after three months.'

(This means the details of the design and all the options are still open whilst the service is still in 'paper' form so that changes can be made or the project abandoned without spending a significant amount of money.)

4 May 1991: Strategic specification (Prepared by Amy)

1. The service will be called 'Come Clean'.
2. This will be a new service.
3. The trigger for the service is 'situation opportunity' but we are also aware that there is 'market pull'.

    To visit the customer's premises to do cleaning. The equipment will be carried in a small van and each service call will be programmed to take half a day.
5. To clean carpets and upholstery.
6. Needs:
    - carpets and upholstery must be clean.
    - colours must not run, fade, change.
    - cleaning must not leave stains or 'tide marks'.
    - there must be no shrinkage.
    - chemicals used must not be harmful (to people or pets).
    - work guaranteed.

    Wants:
    - cleaning done during the week and on Saturday.
    - furniture moved in and out by us.
    - carpets dry in short time – i.e. same day.
    - 'stain guard' applied.
    - no chemical smells.
    - job done punctually (we come when we say we will come).
    - carpets, upholstery, curtains cleaned in one session.
    - other cleaning services offered.
7. The reason for the service is to provide a business opportunity for Carol and Amy. To provide them with a living wage initially which will grow to enable them to have an improving standard of living.
8. 700 cleaning service calls in the first year; 900 calls in the second year; 1,200 calls in the third year.

9.   Including wages, van running costs, depreciation, etc., the running costs will be about £35.50 for each half-day clean.
10. The service to be designed as far as the start of the development stage by 29 June 1991. The service to be in operation by 1 August 1991.
11. The maximum total budget for completion up to the start of the service to be £5,000.
12. Financial return unaltered. That is, £18,000 minimum profit in the first year (wages).
13. Pay off all initial expenditure inside 36 months.
14. Both Amy and Carol to spend 50 hours each week on the project from today until 1 June, when the situation will be reappraised.
15. This project takes top priority over any other job projects.
16. We certainly have the available personnel to run our two-man service. If we expand and need more people, I have some friends who might be interested in joining us.

Layer 3

18 May 1991: Relevant innovations

The tight timescale doesn't allow us scope to innovate with this service. On the face of it the existing concept seems secure but I have been in contact with Alan Hallam and asked him if there is anything on the horizon that might be relevant.

For some time he has been keeping a broad look at all the possible new ideas that could be used for cleaning carpets. He has been to some quite unusual exhibitions, such as Techmart, and read widely (innovation seeking).

He has identified quite an interesting new product, called 'Stainlogon'. It was invented in this country and was announced in a scientific journal. Apparently it is still early in development and it could be three to five years before it comes on the market. He has written a report about it.

Logostat Manufacturing Corporation
The company, Logostat Manufacturing Corporation, has a revolutionary new consumer product to be manufactured in Europe.

The product
The product 'Stainlogon' is an electronic stain remover, removing stains from clothes, carpets and furniture. It is portable and rechargeable from a plug-in wall fixture (as with some small vacuum cleaners and power drills) and is filled with a special cleaning solution. It will remove all stains except paint and can be used on any colour-fast dyed materials. It removes stains only, it does not purify or kill germs (sterilize).

The product will initially retail at £600 but this will fall to £350 after a couple of years when they have got the manufacturing process more efficient. One half-litre bottle of cleaning solution will retail at £5 and will do approximately 40 stains of 10 cm diameter. A bottle of the solution has a shelf life of two years.

Mode of operation
The product works by a form of photochemical reaction that draws the stain towards a light source.

The unit is 25 cm square and 10 cm high. When charged up the unit is placed with the 'hot spot' over the stain. This is similar to the lens of a torch and is fitted with a torch bulb that illuminates the area to be cleaned. Alternatively the unit can be hand held during operation.

When located over the stain the 'on' button is pressed down and held down for a period of 20 seconds. After treatment there is a slight smell of ammonia which fades in about 1 minute.

Apart from filling with fluid and changing worn out rechargeable batteries, the unit is anticipated to be maintenance free.

Technical details
Anticipated demand in Europe will be 2,000 in the first year and 5,000 in subsequent years. It is, therefore, to be mass produced.

The new product has been assembled using components as follows:

- The unit is housed in an injection moulded ABS (plastic) box that consists of a hollow container 10 cm deep and a flat lid held in with four recessed chrome plated screws. The lid has a sliding hatch to obtain access to the two batteries.
- The torch lens and bulb are to be bought in, as is the operating button (60p).
- Inside the unit is an electronic circuit board, to be assembled in-house (£130) from bought-in components (£73) from the Far East.
- The fluid tank measures 125 cm and is filled through a screw plug.
- The cleaning fluid will be bought in, in bulk, from a UK supplier and bottled into half-litre bottles and labelled in-house.
- Other components are to be made in-house, with the exception of the charger socket and rechargeable batteries (2 × HP2) which will be bought in at a cost of £5 from Germany.
- The injection-moulded wall-bracket will be made in-house from polypropylene at a cost of £12.25.
- Manufacturing price is £240 for the unit and £1 for a half-litre bottle of cleaning solution.

'Well that will not be a threat for about five years. It could even be an opportunity if we keep an eye on the product's development and be one of the first on the market to use it.'

18 May 1991: Competition analysis

All the competition seem to operate in the same way, having a maximum service radius of five miles. Only three companies will overlap our 'patch'. They are:

1. *Apex Service Cleaners.* These are part of a larger company but are pretty large themselves. They are based two miles away. They are part of Factory Cleaners that also have a department that does home cleaning. They have four operatives, each with a van, and each operative undertakes two site cleans per day. Typical price £50 inc. VAT. They have about 55 per cent of the local market. The holding company is pretty rigid in its outlook only allowing any changes that fit the overall company objectives. Their main strengths are:

- Their good reputation.
- A guarantee against colour fading.
- Good insurance cover against damage.

Their main weaknesses are:
- A high price.
- They tend to be unreliable about turning up at the appointed time.
- Their equipment is better suited for factory cleaning, rather 'heavy duty'.
- They sometimes send YTS workers to do the job.

2. *Uniclean.* Two men in partnership each with a van and two machines. They seem pretty good and operate from a lock-up garage some eight miles away, so they only overlap part of our proposed operation. Typical price £44 inc. VAT. They have about 35 per cent of the local market. Their main strengths are:

- Very reliable.
- Pleasant and polite.
- Always punctual.
- Will do evening work.

Their main weaknesses are:
- A two-week waiting time for an appointment.
- They will not work at weekends.
- Carpets have 'chemical smell' for a long time.
- Difficult to contact them to make appointment.

3. *New Pin Cleaners.* This seems to be a haphazard operation run by one

man, who also runs a one-man taxi service. He seems to run the cleaning service as a sideline and spends about one day each week on it. He operates from home, half a mile away, and is very inexpensive – £37 inc. VAT. He has about 10 per cent of the local market. Their main strengths are:

- Cheap service.
- Does job quickly.
- Cheerful personality.
- East to contact (phone in van and taxi).

Their main weaknesses are:

- No weekend or evening work.
- Very chatty (although may be a strength – as some clients like this).
- Not reliable.
- Will not move furniture (elderly customers find this a disadvantage).
- Guarantee not offered.

Looking outside our range the average price in London is about £46.

Apart from these there is one other competitor, Rentall Do-It-Yourself, who rent cleaning machines on a collect and return basis. There are two of these in our area. I don't know how much of the local market is taken up by rented machines.

None of the competition seem in any way to be innovative.

Layer 4

23 May 1991: Screening and product definition meeting

Carol to Amy: 'The reports look good and we both agree the business looks like a "goer" (management commitment). It is within our budget (financial control). We can make a satisfactory living from it and still have enough revenue to plough back into the business. For a start those machines and the van will not last forever and our immediate aim should be to buy another couple of cleaning machines. From your estimation we will not be meeting the full market potential of DIY cleaning and we need back-up machines, if only as a safeguard against one of our existing machines breaking down (expansion potential). Another van would greatly increase our flexibility to deliver, but that will have to wait for at least another year.

'The sales and distribution aspects are fine and Alan Hallam will give us a day's training on how to use and maintain them. He reckons it only takes 20 minutes to learn how to operate them (experience and technology can be obtained).

'I think we can write the product definition.'

30 May 1991: Product definition

Prepared by Amy (typically 1,500 words):

The company, Come Clean, will be a service to clean carpets and furniture upholstery, visiting customers/clients homes.

The anticipated price is £46.00 inc. VAT.

The service will operate from a spare room in Carol's house in Chiswick. The room is equipped with a telephone, desk, chair and filing cabinet.

The cleaning equipment will, initially, consist of four steam cleaners and cleaning fluid. Generally it will take, on average, one bottle of cleaning fluid each service call. The steam cleaners will fit into the back of a 15 cwt van.

The range of the service will be a five-mile radius and will operate as follows:

- The service will operate between Tuesday and Saturday inclusive.
- Each morning at 8.30 the two operatives will leave from Carol's house and drive to the first of the morning's appointments, where one will be dropped off to do the cleaning. The second will drive to the next appointment. On completion of the work the second operative will return to the first address and pick up the first operative and equipment in the van.
- After lunch the procedure will be repeated for the two afternoon appointments and the two operatives will return to Carol's house at 5.00 p.m.

One day each week will be allocated to servicing the machines and undertaking general administration, such as accounts.

The competition have been described and all operate in a similar manner to that proposed for Come Clean.

The launch date is to be 1 August 1991.

1 June 1991: Phone call from Carol to Amy:
'I've read the latest service definition and it seems fine, except for a few things. If we are to be out all day we will miss out on any new orders. Therefore, I think we need an answerphone on which we can leave details of price and our availability and customers can place orders. Secondly, supposing we make a blunder on a job and shrink a carpet, we had better include some insurance cover. Even with these extras we are still within our budget. Third, each day one of us could deliver one of the machines to a 'do-it-yourself' customer and we could collect it late afternoon. Who knows, perhaps we will find our DIY customers will be greater than service cleaning and we could spend the day with our feet up? Could you do some more market research into this please?' (Product enrichment/added value.)

7 June 1991: Phone call from Amy to Carol:

'I've done that extra market research on the DIY cleaning, asking around and a few discreet calls on numbers in the *Yellow Pages* and on various leaflets I've collected. It seems that we could expect 30 per cent extra requests to be DIY cleaning (210) and, generally, the users only want the machine for half a day. I've also got some more information on the competition. I will put all these in a report to you.'

9 June 1991: Amy's report – competition analysis (iteration)

It seems most companies only operate on a section of their five-mile radius each day to cut down on travel time. This means that the competition is not as fierce as first thought and Uniclean only enter our proposed operating range all day on Wednesdays and Thursday mornings. We must also cut down on our range if we are also to deliver machines to the DIY customers so I have divided up our area on the attached figure (Fig. 13.1), which will reduce travelling a great deal. Rentall Do-It-Yourself rent their machines for £15 for each day and do most of their renting on Saturday so we will be operating on the most lucrative day. The research shows that we can charge £19 (£21.85 inc. VAT) for the convenience of delivery. If we can achieve the 30 per cent demand for rented machines that could mean an increase in turnover of £4,585 each year including tax.

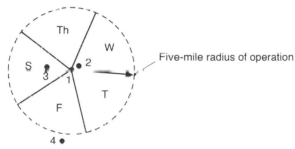

1. Come Clean: operation Tuesday to Saturday
2. New Pin (half mile from Come Clean): one day operation per week
3. Apex (two miles from Come Clean)
4. Uniclean (eight miles from Come Clean): operating Monday to Friday

Segments of operation:
T = Tuesday
W = Wednesday
Th = Thursday
F = Friday
S = Saturday

Fig. 13.1 Operating range.

Insurance
I have got various quotes for cover for damage to the carpets and found one that looks attractive. It will cover both of us for any damage we cause in the office or at customers' homes for £1,000 per year.

Answerphone
These are available in lots of places and a good one will only cost £150.

Neither of these additional expenditures need change our agreed charges and can come out of the money we set aside for the service design and will just avoid us having to borrow. In subsequent years we will have to take the insurance out of profits.

Layer 5

11 June 1991: Meeting

Amy to Carol: 'I think we now know enough to be able to answer the status questionnaires. I have had a go at this and I have put the results in a memo.'

(*Note:* As this is a new business there is unlikely to be a 'service audit' except of individual skills and experience.)

Memo: Find product status

I have filled in the questionnaires. Fortunately, being such a new business we can be flexible and dynamic and so, as expected, we can match the status of our company to that of the market. Anyway, at present, as 'Stainlogon' is still some years off, there appears to be little to alter the status of such a service from being static. I will re-do these questionnaires every six months (periodic check on product status) to make sure that things don't alter.

I have also answered the questionnaire as if we were Apex Cleaners and they don't look as if they will be changing in the forseeable future (status questionnaire used for competition analysis). As you see, Apex are a pretty static company so I doubt if any new innovations will emanate from them. But as we are capable of being dynamic we can move when the market looks like changing. Also, as we have identified the next likely innovation in 'Stainlogon' we can watch developments and move at the optimum time to maximize our benefit from this opportunity. We will probably be offering this service before Apex and the others have even discovered that it exists.

'Come clean'

QUESTIONNAIRE: MACRO-PRODUCT STATUS		
Product type under consideration: COME CLEAN		
Comparison with which product:		
Place a tick in the relevant column:	YES (Static)	NO (Dynamic)
1. If there hasn't been any technical advance recently that may be used to replace this service tick the 'Yes' column and go on to Question 6. If there has, name it and tick the 'No' column.	✔	
2. Is there a large infrastructure based on the existing design that *cannot* be used with the new design (e.g. fuel, sales, spares, distribution, servicing, skills, etc.)? Give one tick in the 'Yes' column for each, or one tick in the 'No' column if there are none.		
3. Are there any conformance standards for this service that cannot be met by the new design?		
4. Put a tick in the 'No' column for every *two* advantages of the technical advance that would make a customer change from the existing service (one tick for lower price). '.		
5. Put one tick in the 'Yes' column for every *two* disadvantages that would make a customer prefer the existing service.		
6. Are a few relatively large organizations dominating this service market? (Tick the 'No' column if any technical advance mentioned in Question 1 comes from one of these organizations.)		✔
7. Do most organizations appear to copy each other?	✔	
8. Has the service been available in its present form for more than five years?	✔	

191

9.	Tick the 'Yes' column if the number of your competitors is decreasing or remaining the same. Tick the 'No' column if the number of your competitors has increased.	✓	
10.	Recently there may have been changes in the economic climate, legislation or resources that make the existing service more or less viable to consumers. Tick the 'Yes' column if these changes have made the existing service more viable or more attractive to customers. Tick the 'No' column if these changes have made the existing service less viable or less attractive to customers. (If neither leave blank.)	✓	
	The market appears to be pretty static at the moment. TOTAL	5	1

Results
An equal number of ticks in both columns or a surplus of ticks in the 'Yes' column indicates that the product status is probably static. A surplus of ticks in the 'No' column indicates that the service status is probably dynamic or potentially dynamic. Knowledge of this status can direct your emphasis in design.

Fig. 13.2 Questionnaire: Macro-product status

QUESTIONNAIRE: MICRO-ORGANIZATION STATUS Service name: COME CLEAN		
Place a tick in the relevant column:	YES (Static)	NO (Dynamic)
1. Does this service interface with other services or product assemblies not made by your organization?		✓
*2. Do you/will you use much dedicated machinery in this service?	✓	
*3. Do you/will you use CAD for the design of this service?		✓

*4. Does your organization have a greater market share or turnover than most of your competitors (or potential competitors)?		✔
**5. Is a fast design time one of the three most important considerations when embarking on a new design?	✔	
**6. Must new designs use the existing sales force and/or distribution networks?	✔	
**7. Must new designs use the existing facilities?	✔	
**8. Must tried and proven methods be used in the design of new services?		✔
**9. Must new designs be an extension of the existing product range?		✔
10. Is this service made by assembling components, the majority of which are made by other organizations?		✔
11. Has the service design specification remained significantly unaltered recently by the market research department and by your main customers?	✔	
12. Do you use the same components from this service in several other services?		✔
Come Clean are dynamic but can operate in a static market. TOTAL	5	7

*If a 'Yes' answer is given to these questions it is in your organization's interests and advantage to seek static services.
**'Yes' answers to these questions suggest that your organization is restricting design to static design. Is this necessary or sensible?

Fig. 13.3 Questionnaire: Micro-organization status.

193

QUESTIONNAIRE: MICRO-ORGANIZATION STATUS

Service name: APEX CLEANERS (competition analysis)

Place a tick in the relevant column:	YES (Static)	NO (Dynamic)
1. Does this service interface with other services or porduct assemblies not made by your organization?	✔	
*2. Do you/will you use much dedicated machinery in this service?	✔	
*3. Do you/will you use CAD for the design of this service?		✔
*4. Does your organization have a greater market share or turnover than most of your competitors (or potential competitors)?	✔	
**5. Is a fast design time one of the three most important considerations when embarking on a new design?		
**6. Must new designs use the existing sales force and/or distribution networks?	✔	
**7. Must new designs use the existing facilities?	✔	
**8. Must tried and proven methods be used in the design of new services?		✔
**9. Must new designs be an extension of the existing product range?	✔	
10. Is this service made by assembling components, the majority of which are made by other organizations?		✔

194

11.	Has the service design specification remained significantly unaltered recently by the market research department and by your main customers?	✓	
12.	Do you use the same components from this service in several other services?	✓	
	Apex Cleaners are static. TOTAL	8	3

Fig. 13.4 Questionnaire: Micro-organization status (competition analysis).

=========================== **Layer 6** ===========================

18 June 1991: Preliminary technical specification

1. Inform Inland Revenue that we are now self-employed for tax purposes.
2. Open an account at the bank for Come Clean and register our signatures so that we can both sign cheques, etc. Get cheque book and pay-in book.
3. Arrange for our National Insurance contributions to be paid from our business account by direct debit every month.
4. Contact an accountant (ask if any of our colleagues can recommend someone).
5. Insurance copy will be required for the van, machinery and for cover in case of accidents to customers carpets and/or furniture. Also for ourselves.
6. We must be reliable, turn up on the day and at the time of the appointments.
7. Our work must be of the highest quality – no colour fading, running, staining or shrinkage.
8. Launch date of 1 August 1991.
9. All appointments made within two weeks of call.
10. No unpleasant chemical smells lingering after cleaning. We can achieve this with the fluid we will be using.
11. No chemicals to be used which are harmful to people or pets. Likewise, I've checked the cleaning fluid and, basically, it is harmless.
12. Electric points needed on site for our machines (they cannot run off the van battery).
13. Four two-year-old carpet/upholstery cleaning machines and other bits and pieces for £800.
14. One second-hand 15 cwt van, insured, taxed and with MOT certificate.

I've located a good one for £2,000. I can put transfers of the company name on the side. Annual running costs will be £900.

15. Cleaning fluid in three batches of 60 bottles at £1 per bottle.

16. Two operatives (us).

17. Headed notepaper, business cards etc. can be ordered when we are more established.

18. Maintenance will take place during quiet periods. About 10 hours per month will cover this. Most maintenance we can do ourselves but once each year the machines will require a major service done by the manufacturers. This takes one week and costs £35 for each machine. We can have that done during our summer holiday (if we can fit one in!). We will need two new machines in two years (£400 each) and another second-hand van in four years. We will be able to afford these when the time comes with the amount we will be earning.

19. There are no problems in disposing of any of the things we will be using in the business when that time comes. Pollution is not a problem either.

20. £35.50 is the final cost for us to provide each site visit, including wages, and we will charge £40 + VAT (£46).

21. We can practise and 'perfect our act' in the time up until 1 August. My carpets could do with a good clean, after some tests on some dumped carpets.

(The preliminary technical specification given above is only a brief outline to give a 'flavour' of the type of things to be included. The same is true of the following preliminary marketing specification.)

18 June 1991: Preliminary marketing specification

1. We shall promote our product by delivering handbills to all houses in our area of operation. Advertise in local (free) newspaper, and in newsagents' windows. I'm writing a press release about two girls starting a business on their redundancy pay which the local rag says they will print. You will do a good promotional tape for the answerphone. Consider *Yellow Pages* and *Thompson Directories* later.

2. The van will look good with the transfers on the side, as long as we keep it clean.

3. Please get the name of the company written on the pocket of our overalls.

4. Organize printing of handbills to be delivered with local newspapers.

5. At £46 per clean our price is competitive, not the cheapest (£37) nor the most expensive (£50).

6. The promotion will start during the last week of July ready for the service launch on 1 August 1991.

7. We will offer a carpet and upholstery cleaning service. This will be in

two forms. A half-day visit to clients' homes to do the cleaning and a 'do-it-yourself' hire service with us delivering and collecting the equipment.

8. We will operate on a radius of five miles (the most we can hope to manage) and operate a diary so that we only visit certain areas on certain days of the week. This is the normal practice of the competition. The van will be ideal for this service.

9. The service will be fully insured and, therefore, guaranteed.

10. We will ensure a visit within two weeks of an order.

11. We will endeavour to give a happy, polite and personable service. We must appear to be the most efficient attentive, and well trained outfit.

12. For the hire service we will need to give some 'training'. It will be sufficient to provide an instruction leaflet and I will have one written in the next couple of weeks. We can see if it works when my mum comes to visit next month.

13. The high interest rate means that people are buying fewer carpets at present and, because of the high mortgage rate, are not moving house as often. As a result they are cleaning the carpets they own more. There is no sign of a change in this for the next two years.

14. The life of this service looks assured for the next five years, at least.

15. We will undertake 704 service calls per year. We can also do 210 equipment hires at £21.85 per half day (turnover over £32,000 before VAT).

16. I have not discovered anything new about the competition. My original reports are still correct.

17. The anticipated demand seems to be so great at this time that we are only limited by what we can do. If this forecast proves to be correct we can either expand by employing some help or put up our prices until supply matches demand. We should consider this situation every six months.

'So far so good, Carol. I cannot see much standing in the way of us having a successful service on our hands. We have considered all the important areas and even allowing for the compromises everything still seems to hold together. And what is more we haven't spent much of our money yet.'

(*Note* the deliberate overlap between the technical and marketing specifications to show the areas of possible conflict between parties with differing interests.)

'I think we can go into the next layer and write our service design specification. We had better move pretty fast if we are going to cover all the elements in sufficient depth and be in a position to know if we want to buy the cleaning equipment by the end of June.'

197

'Don't panic Amy. The SDS will just be a compilation of what information we have already collected with the addition of a few missing bits. There will also be some more compromises to agree on, but that shouldn't cause too many problems.'

Layer 7

25 June 1991: Assemble full service design specification

In the case of a new business like Come Clean, this will be their business plan. This would include a greater emphasis on financial projections, which have not been included in this book. (The service design specification will be a combination of the subspecifications so far compiled with all additional elements considered. The SDS has not been compiled for this example.)

'I've worked out our costs, Carol, and looks as if we are still on course:

Initial expenditure:

	£
Van	2,000
Insurance	1,000
Cleaning machines	800
Promotion	200
Answerphone	150
Cleaning fluid	60

Total £4,210 inside the initial target of £5,000.

Anticipated first year income about:

	£
700 service cleans at £40 per clean (ex. VAT)	28,000
200 delivery DIY cleans at £19 per clean (ex. VAT)	3,800
Total	£31,800

Surplus for the first year £31,800 – £4,210 = £27,590

Take from this:	
	£
Our £9,000 salary each	18,000
Van running costs	900
National Insurance etc.	3,000
Cleaning fluid	700
Machine maintenance: 4 × £35	140
Total	£22,740

'This gives us £4,850 to plough back into the business such as towards the van and new machines.'

'Honestly Amy, the figures are all right but that's not what I call a financial spreadsheet. Add to our initial expenditure the price of a good, simple book on keeping accounts.'

═══════════════ **Layer 8** ═══════════════

28 June 1991: Concept design

'As the service appears to be static, in this case there is no need to consider new concepts. The new innovation is some way off and we are keeping an eye on that, the existing concept is the right one to use. We can now embark on the high cost stages of the design process. Up to now we have not spent much money but we have spent a good deal of our time,' said Amy.

'Yes, but we have organised the early stages of the design process as it should be done. We can proceed with the later, high-cost, part as sure as one can be that "Come Clean" will be a success. Not having just drifted into the service design we are more certain that we won't squander our redundancy pay', answered Carol. 'We can now telephone Alan Hallam and tell him we look like having a sucessful business and we want to buy his cleaning machines.'

'All this talk of success has given me an appetite. Fancy a pizza?'

Appendix

A discussion of
definitions of design

The process of design is, perhaps, new to many people employed in the service sector. As a result, in this appendix, we describe how others have defined or described the word 'design'.

McLeod (1969) said that 'design is concerned with making things people want'. This fact is fundamental to the whole consideration of the subject. Jean Eric Aubert (1985) expanded on this definition by stating that 'design starts with the definition of the product's objectives, then is concerned with the whole coherence of the product to meet its objective.'

Looking at the definitions for 'design' the majority tend not to go far enough, stopping at the point of production. As Oakley (1984) states: 'Unfortunately many companies believe that design stops at the launch of a new product', and many definitions of design appear to do the same, for example design is the 'nature of the problem-solving task required to convert an idea into a new product' (Parker 1982). This definition also fails to mention the market need.

The following definition, by Ken Wallace for British Standards (1986), starts off well: 'Design is the process of converting an idea or market need into the detailed information from which a product can be made.'

Another failing with the above definitions is that the multidisciplinary nature of design is not mentioned, for example design is 'the preparation of solutions to problems concerning creating, producing and marketing products' (CNAA 1984). This definition also ignores the market need, a known failure of many designs. A much better definition, covering most aspects and implying the multidisciplinary nature of design but not actually stating it, is one by SEED (1985a) which says 'Design is seen as the total activity necessary to provide an artifact to meet a market need, it commences with the identification of the need and is not complete until the resulting product is in use.'

The above definition does acknowledge that design does not cease when the product enters production, as does the following definition, which eliminates consideration of market need. 'The designer's responsibility covers the whole process from conception to the issue of detailed instruction for production and his interest continues throughout the life of the product in service' (MTIRA 1984).

Iteration is an important part of design. Almost all practitioners accept the need to reappraise continually that which has gone before in the design process, but we have only found one definition that mentions iteration:

> The design process involves iterative decision-making. The solution to a problem results from making and implementing a long series of large and small decisions. These decisions fall into two major categories,
> (1) planning decisions that determine the course of the design process and
> (2) technical decisions that determine the actual design solution.
>
> (Dixon and Simmons (1983)

Apart from mentioning iteration the definition is far too long and again ignores the market research and selling ends of the process. It also does not mention a 'product'. We have found that design without a 'product' is worthless and, therefore, it should be mentioned in any definition of design.

Summarizing, we believe that any definition of design should include the following:

1. An indication of market need (market pull) or an idea (technical push).
2. It should describe its multidisciplinary nature.
3. It should state that it is an iterative process.
4. It must mention that its purpose is to produce a 'product' (and a service is a product).
5. It must state that it continues beyond the start of production.

Design management has also been defined by writers. The earliest was Farr (1966) who described it as 'the function of defining a design problem, finding the most suitable designer and making it possible for him (or her) to solve it on time and within an agreed budget'. The management of design has progressed a lot further since that was written, design teams being the most obvious difference.

Glossary

Terms used in this book

Concept vulnerability. Where a product is treated as static when it is potentially dynamic, or the concept chosen is under threat from a 'better' product concept (such as an innovation), or when the wrong concept is chosen. (Derived from Pugh 1981.)

Design disciplines. Those professional activities which are to be found in the design and process of a service.

Design management. The management of (service) design is the planning, organization and control of money, labour, materials and time to achieve the objectives of the project. (SEED 1985a.)

Design review. A formal, documented, comprehensive and systematic examination of the capability of a design to meet the service design specification, to identify problems and propose solutions. They should be held whenever necessary and involve all who can make a contribution.

Disposal. The end of the design process.

Dynamic design. A service design where changes are (or should be) innovative. The service concept is likely to change.

Dynamic process design. Product, service or distribution activities that do not appear in the service audit.

Elements. The areas of investigation that are included in the service design specification.

Ergonomics. 'The scientific study of the relationship between man and his environment' (Murrell 1969).

Evolutionary (or incremental) design. Continuous product improvement to meet slowly changing market needs or evolving science and technology aimed at sustaining or expanding existing markets (Parker 1980).

Indication of success or failure. Would you have liked your money invested in it?

Industrial design. That part of design that deals with the outward appearance of a product, including graphics.

Innovation. The process of taking an invention forward into the first marketable product.

Invention. The act of insight by which a new and promising technical possibility is recognized and worked out (at least mentally and perhaps physically) in its essential, most rudimentary form (Schener 1971).

Iteration. Backtracking to check or update the information that has been collected earlier in the process.

Just-in-Time (JIT). To produce and deliver finished goods just in time to be sold, subassemblies just in time to be assembled into finished goods, fabricated parts just in time to go into subassemblies, and purchased materials just in time to be transformed into fabricated parts (Schonberger 1982).

Marketing. The management function responsible for identifying, anticipating and satisfying customer requirements profitably (The Institute of Marketing).

Mechanistic communication. Pyramid type of communication and organizational chart, where direction is by formal rules. In this system problems can be broken down into specialisms 'as if it were the subject of a subcontract' (Burns and Stalker 1961).

Organic communication. This system has a more 'lateral' type of communication and 'tends to resemble lateral consultation rather than vertical command' (Burns and Stalker 1961).

Parallel processing. Design and implementation processes that can be undertaken concurrently.

Product status A term used to describe static or dynamic products (Pugh 1983).

Quality. 'The totality of features and characteristics of a product or service that bear on its total ability to satisfy a given need' (BS 4778: 1979 *Quality Assurance*).

Quality circles. Small groups of employees who meet regularly to solve problems and find ways of improving aspects of their work (Institute of Quality Assurance).

Quota sample. A sample that conforms to a pre-selected criterion, e.g., education, age, salary, etc.

Random sample. A sample which is taken on a 'first come, first served' basis.

Reliability. The ability of an item to perform a required function under stated conditions for a given period of time (ISO 8402: 1986).

Services or service products. Activities, benefits or satisfactions which are offered for sale, or provided in connection with the sale of goods (The American Marketing Association 1960).

Service audit The existing capabilities of the organization and their main sub-contractors.

Service concept. The outcome of the creative thinking process.

Service design specification. A definitive document specifying the requirements and attributes to which the resulting service should conform. (Derived from SEED 1985b.)

Simultaneous engineering. A concurrent activity on the design and manufacturing aspects of a product, resulting in enhanced quality of the design output with minimal duplication (S.C. Miller, Director-Engineering, Rolls Royce plc).

Skills audit. A glossary of knowledge, abilities and training of those involved in the design of a product or service.

Standard. A technical specification approved by a recognized national, international or company standardizing body for repeated or continuous application (BSI).

Static design. A product design where changes are (or should be) incremental or non-existent. The concept is unlikely to change.

Static plateau. The period of time after a dominant innovation where design changes are incremental.

Static process design. Product, service or distribution activities that appear in the service audit.

Trigger. That which instigates the start of the design process.

Total quality management. The application of continuous improvement to quality in all aspects throughout an organization.

Total Service Design. A multidisciplinary, iterative process that takes an idea and/or market need forward into implementation or selling. Total design must include all aspects up to the point of product disposal.

References

Adams, James L. (1987) *Conceptual Blockbusting: A Guide to Better Ideas.* Harmondsworth: Penguin.

Alexander, M. (1985) Creative Marketing and Innovative Consumer Product Design. *Design Studies,* Vol. 6.

American Marketing Association, Committee on Definitions (1960) *Marketing Definitions: A Glossary of Marketing Terms,* AMA.

Archer, B. (1986) Conference Reports. *Design Studies,* Vol. 7, No. 2, p. 113.

Aubert, J. E. (1985), in Langdon, R. and Rothwell, R. (eds) (1985) *Design and Innovation: Policy and Management.* Francis Pinter.

Black, J. (1989) Colloquium: Research in Engineering Design, Institution of Electrical Engineers, London.

Blumberg, D. (1989) *The Consultant Forum,* Vol. 5, No. 1.

Boddy, D. and Buchanan, D. A. (1986) *Managing New Technology.* Blackwell.

BS 7000 (1989) *Guide to Managing Product Design.* London: British Standards Institute.

BSI (forthcoming) *Guide to the Preparation of Specifications.* London: British Standards Institute.

Buggie, F. D. (1981) *New Product Development Strategies.* Amarcom.

Burns, T. and Stalker, G. M. (1961) *The Management of Innovation.* London: Tavistock.

Buzan, T. (1984) *Use Your Head.* BBC. (Revised and extended edition.)

Cane, A. (1990) Executives found ignorant of data processing. *Financial Times,* 8 February.

Clipson, C. (1988) *Design Management.* Open University Business School, Tutorial Tape 1.

CNAA, Department of Trade and Industry and the Design Council (1984) *Managing Design: An Initiative in Management Education.* London: Design Council.

Cook, P. (1990) The business of innovation: an interview with Paul Cook, *Harvard Business Review,* March – April.

Cooper, R. G. (1983) A process model for industrial new product development. *IEEE Transactions of Engineering Management,* Vol. EM30, No. 1, pp. 2 – 11.

Cooper, R. G. (1988) The new product process: A decision guide for management. *Journal of Marketing Management,* Vol. 3, No. 3, pp. 238 – 55.

Corfield, K. G. (Chairman) (1979) *Product Design.* London: NEDO.

Courtis, J. (1988) *Marketing Services: A Practical Guide.* British Institute of Management/Kogan Page.

Cowell, D. W. (1984) *The Marketing of Services.* London: Heinemann.

References

Crimp, M. (1990) *The Marketing Research Process,* 3rd ed. Prentice-Hall.

Crockenburg, S. B. (1972) Creativity tests: a boon or boon doggle for education? *Review of Educational Research* 42: pp. 27–45, 361.

Davidson, H. (1976) *Offensive Marketing.* Harmondsworth: Penguin.

De Bono, E. (1982) *Lateral Thinking for Management: A Handbook.* Harmondsworth: Penguin.

de Newtown, J. (1990) Exploiting the Opportunity. In *Successfully Managing Product Development.* Hawkesmere Seminar, 20–21 March.

Design Council (1985) *Innovation. A Study of the Problems and Benefits of Product Innovation.* London: Design Council.

Dixon, J. R. and Simmons, M. K. (1983) Computers that design: expert systems for mechanical engineers. *Computers in Mechanical Engineering,* November.

Drucker, P. F. (1985) *Innovation and Entrepreneurship.* London: Heinemann.

Duffy, J. and Kelly, J (1989) United front is faster. *Management Today,* November, pp. 131–9.

Farr, M. (1966) *Design Management.* London: Hodder & Stoughton.

Foster, R. N. (1986) *Innovation – The Attacker's Advantage.* McKinscy and Co. Ltd, p. 134.

Foxall, G. R. (1984) *Corporate Innovation: Marketing and Strategy.* London: Croom Helm.

Francis, A. and Winstanley, D. (1989) Managing new product development: some alternative ways to organize the work of technical specialists. *Journal of Marketing Management,* Vol. 4, No. 2.

Freeman, C. (1988). Seminar: The New Technology Paradigm and the Future of the European Economy, Polytechnic of Central London, 25 November 1988.

Fullan, M. (1970) Industrial technology and worker integration in the organization. *American Sociological Review,* Vol. 35, pp. 1028–39.

Gregory, S. (1966) *The Design Method.* London: Butterworths

Guardian Obituaries, 17 April 1989.

Guildford, J. P. and Hoepfner, R. (1971) *The Analysis of Intelligence.* New York: McGraw-Hill.

Haire, M. (1950) Projective techniques in marketing research. *Journal of Marketing,* Vol. 11, pp. 649 56.

Harper, M. (1961) A new profession to aid management. *Journal of Marketing.*

Herriot, P. (1984) *Down from the Ivory Tower: Graduates and their Jobs.* Chichester: Wiley.

Herzberg, F., Mausner, B. S. and Snyderman, G (1959) *The Motivation to Work.* New York: Wiley.

Hollins, W. J. (1978) 'Reducing an R&D Work Mountain'. DMS Project, unpublished.

Hollins, W. J. (1988) Product status and the management of design. *Engineering Designer,* Vol. 14, No. 4, pp. 13–15.

Hollins, W. J. (1989) *Product Status and the Management of Product Design.* PhD Thesis, University of Strathclyde.

Hollins, W. J. and Pugh, S. (1990) *Successful Product Design: What to do and When.* London: Butterworths.

Humble, J. and Jones, G. (1989) Creating a climate for innovation. *Long Range Planning,* Vol. 22, No. 4, pp. 46–51.

Jewkes, J., Sawyers, D. and Stillerman, R. (1969) *The Sources of Invention.* 2nd edn. London: MacMillan.

Johne, F. A. and Snelson, P. A (1988) Success factors in product innovation: A selective review of the literature. *Journal of Product Innovation Management,* Vol. 5, No. 2, pp. 100 – 10.

Jones, J. C. (1970) *Design Methods: Seeds of Human Futures,* 2nd edn. Chichester: Wiley.

Kanter, R. M. (1983) *The Change Masters: Entrepreneurs at Work.* Counterpoint Allen and

Kennaway, A. (1989). Report on Visit to Japan from May – September 1989. Imperial College, London, September 1989.

Unwin (1986). Also titled (1983) *The Change Master: Innovation for Productivity in the American Corporation.* New York: Simon & Schuster.

Klein, B. H. (1977) *Dynamic Economics.* Harvard University Press.

Koberg, D. and Bagnall, J. (1980) *The Universal Traveler.* Los Altos, California: William Kaufmann.

Kotler, P. (1986) *Principles of Marketing,* 3rd edn. Prentice-Hall.

Kotler, P. (1988) *Marketing Management: Analysis, Planning, Implementation and Control,* 6th edn. Prentice-Hall.

Langdon, R. and Rothwell, R. (eds) (1985) *Design and Innovation: Policy and Management.* Francis Pinter.

Leech, D. J. and Turner, B. T. (1985) *Engineering Design for Profit.* Ellis Horwood. Engineering Science Series. Chichester.

Levitt, T. (1960) Marketing Myopia. *Harvard Business Review,* July – August.

Levitt, T. (1981) Marketing intangible products and product intangibles. *Harvard Business Review,* May – June. pp. 94 – 102.

Likert, R. A. (1932) A technique for the measurement of attitudes. *Archives of Psychology,* No. 140.

Lorenz, C. (1983) SIAD Design Management Seminars.

Lovelock, C. H. (1984) *Services Marketing.* Prentice-Hall.

Lovelock, C. H. (1988) *Managing Services.* Prentice-Hall.

Machine Tool Industry Research Association (1984) *Design Manual,* Vol. 1.

Majaro, S. (1990) Innovation and top management. *MBA Review,* Vol. 2. No. 1, March.

McLeod, T. S. (1969) *Management of Research, Development and Designs in Industry.* Gower.

Merle Crawford, C. (1987) *New Product Management,* 2nd edn. Irwin.

Miller, S. C. (1990) *Design for Manufacture and Quality.* London Business School/Design Museum Design Management Seminar, 9 May.

Morton, J. A. (1971) *Organising for Innovation: A Systems Approach to Technical Management.* New York: McGraw-Hill.

Moss, F. (1989) Japanese pursue European ambitions in financial services. *Independent,* 4 October.

Murdick, R. G., Render, B. and Russell, R. S. (1990) *Service Operation Management.* Boston: Allyn and Bacon.

Murrell, K. F. H. (1969) *Ergonomics. Man in his Working Environment,* 2nd edn. Chapman & Hall.

Norton, M. (ed.) (1988) A Guide to Company Giving. 1988 – 89 edition, *Directory of Social Change.*

Oakley, M. (1984) *Managing Product Design.* London: Weidenfeld & Nicolson.

Olins, W. (1989) *Corporate Identity: Making Business Strategy Visible Through Design.* Thames and Hudson.

Osborn, A. (1953) *Applied Imagination.* New York: Scribner.

Osgood, C. E., Succi, G. J. and Tannenbaum, P. H. (1957) *The Measurement of Meaning.* Urbana: University of Illinois Press.

References

O'Shaughnessy, J. (1984) *Competitive Marketing: A Strategic Approach.* Allen & Unwin.

Pahl, G. and Beitz, W. (Wallace, K. (ed.)) (1984) *Engineering Design.* London: The Design Council/Springer-Verlag.

Parker, R. C. (1980) *Guidelines for Product Innovation.* London: BIM.

Parker, R. C. (1982) *The Management of Innovation.* Chichester: Wiley.

Parkes, C. (1989) Time for management to get a grip. *Financial Times,* 30 March.

Parkinson, S. T. (1981) *Successful New Product Development. An International Comparative Study.* Conference R&D Management, University of Strathclyde, 11 February.

Peters, T. J. and Waterman, R. H. (1982). *In Search of Excellence: Lessons from America's best run Companies.* New York: Harper and Row.

Pugh, S. (1981) Design Decision – How to Succeed and Know Why. *Proc. Conf. Engineering Design,* Birmingham, UK.

Pugh, S. (1983) *The Application of CAD in Relation to Dynamic/Static Product Concepts.* Conference, ICED83, Copenhagen, 15–18 August

Rivett, P. and Ackoff, R. E. (1963) *A Manager's Guide to Operational Research.* Chichester: Wiley.

Rothwell, R. (1972) Factors for Success in Industrial Innovations. *Project Sappho – A Comparative Study of Success and Failure in Industrial Innovations.* Sussex: Science Policy Research Unit.

Rothwell, R. (1977) The characteristics of successful innovations. *R&D Management,* Vol. 7, p. 191.

Rothwell, R. and Gardiner, P. (1984) Design and competition in engineering. *Long Range Planning,* Vol. 17, No. 3, pp. 30–91.

Schein, E. H. (1969) *Process Consultation: Its Role in Organization Development.* Addison-Wesley.

Schener, F. M. (1971) *Industrial Market Structure and Economic Performance.* Chicago, IL: Rand McNally.

Schonberger, R. J. (1982) *Japanese Manufacturing Techniques: Nine Hidden Lessons in Simplicity.* New York: Free Press.

SEED (1985a) Curriculum for Design Engineering Undergraduate Course. *Proceedings of the Working Party for Discussion at SEED.*

SEED (1985b) *Shared Experience in Engineering Design,* 2nd Report.

Starr, M. K. (1963) *Product Design and Decision Theory.* Prentice-Hall.

Takeuchi, H. and Nanaka, I. (1986) The new product developmnt game. *Harvard Business Review,* January–February, pp. 137–46.

Thurstone, L. L. (1928) Attitudes can be measured. *American Journal of Sociology,* Vol. 33, pp. 529–54.

Twiss, B. C. (1987) *Managing Technological Innovation,* 3rd edn. Longman.

Urban, G. L., Hauser, J. R. and Dholakin, N. (1987) *Essentials of New Product Management.* Prentice-Hall.

Valery, N. (1989) Japanese Technology Survey, Zeroing In. *The Economist,* 2 December.

Voss, C. (1985) *Operations Management in Service Industries.* Chichester: Wiley.

Wall, R. A. (ed.) (1986) *Finding and Using Product Information.* Gower.

Wallace, K. (1986) QMS4/1/1 Draft Notes, British Standard Subcommittee for the Proposed Standard 'Design Management Systems'. London.

Wallace, K. (1989) Colloquium: Research in Engineering Design. Institution of Electrical Engineers, London.

References

Walsh, V., Roy, R. and Bruce, M. (1988) Competitive by design. *Journal of Marketing Management,* Vol. 4, No. 2, p. 201.

Wilson, A. (1972) *The Marketing of Professional Services.* New York: McGraw-Hill.

Index

Index

Index

market 57
Sunk costs 27–30
Superseded product 22
Supply and demand curve 90–1

Technical journals 126
Technology lag 169
Technology transfer 168–74
Telephone interviews 47
Testing 86, 133
Thinking,
   convergent 71, 73
   divergent 71
Threshold model 71
Thurstone scale method 50–1
Tight timescale 121
Topping up 67, 86
Total Design, definition 10

Total Quality 96–8
Total Service Design, definition 13
Total quality management 96
Training 104, 114, 119, 148–53
   cycle 152
   manager 150
   process 150
   strategy 149
Transfer 74
Trigger 124

Unsuccessful products 173

Variation 166
Visualization 75

Weight 82